THE
WORLD
ACCORDING TO
DOG

AMUSING LIFE LESSONS
TAUGHT TO US BY DOGS

TORI LEVITT

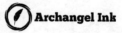

"Dogs do speak, but only to those who know how to listen."
—Orhan Pamuk

This book is dedicated to all dogs that steal our hearts and stoke our souls.

My daily thanks and glory to God through whom all things are possible; and to my pet nannies, who divinely fulfill our purpose at Doolittle's Doghouse.

CONTENTS

INTRODUCTION

If you are a rabid dog fan like me, you understand the indelible enlightenment and joy that only a dog can provide in your daily walk in life.

Notwithstanding dogs with working jobs—those with special training for the police or military, farming, hunting, herding, therapy, and public service—almost all dogs are now embraced as children in the family and are treated similarly. In many cases, the dogs are better behaved.

They demonstrate the same emotions and behaviors we would naturally associate with humans. Dogs experience love, jealousy, attachment, separation anxiety, sadness, loneliness, memory, and—if you're doing it right—genuine happiness in the presence of others.

In order to help a dog feel fully enveloped into your world, embrace the parallel that they are no different than human children who require saintly patience and guidance as they navigate their world inside of yours. Nothing is sacred, including your privacy!

Before you get a dog, understand that they lick everything; themselves then you. They drip and drool. They make messes. They get into your belongings and your bed (because they want to be close to you). They won't draw on the walls with crayons yet might eat them just to be ornery.

They need regular exercise and mental stimulation. They get sick and mark, bark, and barf on occasion. They shed. Despite the touted hypo-allergenic breeds, all dogs shed; it's a matter of degree. There is no non-shedding breed per se; those with curly coats simply trap the hair so it doesn't fall off. Regular grooming is required for these breeds so the coat doesn't mat. If you seriously need a dog that won't shed at all, your best bet is the Hairless Chinese Crested.

If you can accept that there is no perfect dog and are prepared to parent for their lifetime, you will soon discover that Roger A. Caras, wildlife photographer, writer, and preservationist, was right when he said:

> Dogs have given us their absolute all. We are the center of their universe. We are the focus of their love, faith and trust. They serve us in return for scraps. It is, without a doubt, the best deal man has ever made.[1]

This book is not meant to represent know-it-all advice nor compete with experts. We merely wish to share our unique experiences with you in the hope that you gain additional insight regarding these wonderful creatures God created for our sanity.

In a half-insane world, driven primarily by technology, social media, and uncontrollable events, dogs keep us calm and balanced—if we know how to bond with them. You can be their sole object of admiration and reverence and gain a fresh perspective on how dogs think and feel.

As we chase our tails in pursuit of our own happiness, dogs just know how to enjoy each day for what it is, with contentment in your companionship when given reciprocal devotion and respect.

Our lives at Doolittle's Doghouse are devoted primarily to dogs, in the interest of cage-free boarding and in support of their health and wellness—nose to tail. We are not intentionally excluding the companionship benefits of other wonderful animals, including cats,

---

1   "Roger Caras," AZ Quotes, accessed November 23, 2018, https://www.azquotes.com/quote/354035.

pocket pets, feathery friends, reptiles, and other creatures you have invited into your home.

I hope you enjoy similar enlightenment from your own dog and those you will read about as you turn the pages.

The World According to Dog is our version of *Paw & Order*, and these are the dogs' stories.

CHAPTER ONE

A HUMBLE BEGINNING

I was born in Des Moines, Iowa, to two wonderful parents who were kids when they had kids.

My dad was a high school teacher, coach, referee, homebuilder, and property manager—all at the same time. He artfully maintained several jobs to put food on the table, some of which he hunted. But that meant he didn't have spare time to devote to our family dogs. They were kept outside in kennel runs and had minimal family interaction. It never occurred to me to beg to allow them in the house, much less sleep in our beds.

Fortunately, trends in pet ownership have changed for the better, as we now recognize pets as family instead of property.

Fast-forward. As an adult, I got married, became a mom, enjoyed a fruitful career in banking, and thought I had my life nailed—until I was forced to reinvent myself after a divorce and the 2008 real estate crash.

I now pick up dog poop for a living. And I couldn't be happier.

Ten years ago, I began boarding dogs in my home, cage-free, with nary an idea of what I was doing. It just naturally grew from hosting a few friends' dogs with my own to a larger invitation extended to the public. Via word of mouth only, dogs came to live with us when their parents traveled. Nash, my son, was nine years old at the time, and he and his friends became my dog-walking assistants.

We would saddle up and have pet parades around the neighborhood. You've seen the pictures of professional dog walkers with ten dogs on (or off) leash walking in perfect formation. I'm not claiming that was me. Rather, we were a bunch of screwballs twirling around leashes and each other to give the dogs their necessary exercise.

My First Assistants and Dog Walkers

While I continued to finance the then-broken American dream of homeownership, my grass-roots dog boarding service grew.

Four years in, it was common to have ten dogs per day with free roam of the home. I spent most of the day in the backyard with a plastic bag in my hand. Consider the amount of output created by ten dogs twice a day. I had the smelliest receptacle on the block; had I been smarter, I'd have started my own line of fertilizer.

As a fastidious housekeeper unwilling to let the backyard turn into a minefield, I didn't realize the importance of analyzing the "debris" until informed by pet parents of the unusual and sneaky ways their dogs would seek out food in the home. Dogs are natural hunters, so it should be no surprise that anything left within nose reach on a counter or kitchen floor is fair game.

This became relevant when a client delivered her Bull Mastiff, Zoey, who had consumed an entire Easter basket of chocolate, wrappers and all, depriving the kids of the spoils.

Chocolate is toxic to most dogs, yet Zoey topped the scale at 120 pounds, so her girth mitigated the usual concerns. I just needed to be sure Zoey would expel the *foil wrappers* she inhaled, or we would be visiting her vet. Praise the Lord, it all worked out, and I bagged some impressive glitter in the litter, with sufficient confidence that she was safe from bowel obstruction.

Bull Mastiffs are gentle giants whose origins stretch back to the end of the nineteenth century as gamekeepers' sentinels tasked with guarding against poaching on the estate. The goal was to defend and subdue the poachers but not maul them. Their ability to wait silently as the poacher and their dog encroached, then nab the thieves with little harm, became their claim to fame. Zoey had her own poaching style.

And then came Charlie, my favorite Weimaraner, who ate a little boy's shoe before checking in. His parents, Jenny and Kevin, had a toddler in the home, so I imagine there were many objects of desire in Charlie's purview. Ethan's shoe must have been dazzling to Charlie—I found the rainbow of rubber pieces peeking back at me for a week. Again, I mentally sized up the amount of colorful output and felt confident Charlie was out of the woods.

Weimaraners were originally bred in Germany as gundogs that could hunt all types of game, including bigger prey such as deer and bear. Captured in costume and cleverly marketed by the photographer William Wegman, they are aptly described in breed books as "needy." Charlie was no exception in this regard; he was either glued to my side or walking between my legs any time he couldn't be in my lap!

He could fold himself into a ball to squeeze into the twelve inches of remaining couch space next to me.

I don't know what possessed Charlie to hunt and devour his human brother's shoe, although it may have simply resembled a dog toy to him. Some dogs attack their toys as if they were prey.

A common behavior of wild wolf packs is to desecrate the kill, tearing apart the meat, intestines, and bones. It's ancestral. Have you ever wondered if there's an inner wolf in your dog as you surveyed the stuffing all over the floor or the "dead" toys littering your living room?

If you suspect your dog has consumed something foreign after spying suddenly limp and depleted toys, missing socks that the mystical dryer monster didn't consume, or empty wrappers on the floor, carefully analyze their output to make sure it doesn't stay inside too long.

It's A-OK, and even recommended, to peek at every pile, however unnerving it might be to stare at a pile of poop. Be firm in your vigil. A change in texture or color, the appearance of blood or something foreign or alive (parasites), or an object wrapped in film could be a signal of a GI change or condition that requires a vet's analysis.

And if you wonder why your dog is always looking at you while he is conducting his "business" in the backyard, it's because he knows this is a very vulnerable position to be in, and he wants to be sure he's safe in that brief moment. Some dogs can't handle this temporary vulnerability and require complete privacy, so you might need to look the other way.

Zoey & Aunt Saucey

Charlie – the Wanna-Be-A-Lap-Dog Weimaraner

CHAPTER TWO
THE CALL OF NATURE

Born a natural blonde, I needed some "light bulb" moments to hone my skills as a professional pet sitter. Cruiser, a loveable Golden Retriever, was born with a fatal heart condition that made anesthesia or surgery too risky—this included neutering. I accepted that he was an intact male and loved him with all my heart, as he loved every dog and human in his purview.

Maggie, an affable pint-size, five-pound Shih Tzu, arrived the same day that Cruiser was camping out. What I failed to flush out in advance, and Maggie's parents neglected to disclose ahead of time, was that Maggie was in estrus: "Oh, by the way, Maggie is in heat … gotta catch my plane." Really? And she's booked for two weeks?

Maggie was not only in "season," she was ready to party. She danced like I had never seen before. My tiny prancer. Though Cruiser responded to the call of nature, he merely drooled in epic amounts, thanks to his immaturity.

When it dawned on me what was transpiring and perspiring between these two, I separated them with a baby gate and mopped the floors while maintaining constant guard until Cruiser could return home. He was a flummoxed mess. Armed with this new insight, I swiftly revised my client forms to include more probing questions prior to boarding.

Note to any dog owner with an unspayed female: build Fort Knox when she cycles! Any male dog within miles of a female in heat will traverse hill and dale to follow their inherent impulses. I just got lucky that Cruiser didn't jump the gate to break dance with Maggie and create a new breed not likely to be recognized by the American Kennel Club.

Following this idiotic episode, I recognized that I needed to self-educate on a faster track, so I devoured every CD and book written by Cesar Milan, Tamar Geller, Alexandra Horowitz, the Monks of New Skete, and countless other experts, to get inside the dog's mind.

I was especially interested in Ms. Geller's dog-training background, which she successfully developed after first observing wild wolves in Israel. As I've had my own revolving pack of domesticated "wolves" to study over the years, I've learned from all of them. I can say with confidence that dogs lead the pack as the best teachers.

CHAPTER THREE

OBEDIENCE 101—FIRST STARTERS TO AVOID DARTERS

When parenting a dog, it's easy to establish expectations through training, beginning with the simple commands of sit, come, stay, and heel. Any dog can learn to sit for a treat. Coming when called takes more time to teach, as the average dog given off-leash opportunity will find immense entertainment running away from you! Some might think it's a fun game of "catch me if you can!"

Stella was my first furry client and arrived with wild abandon and very few manners. None, actually. Every stick of furniture was playground equipment for her. As a neophyte pet sitter, I had no clue what to do yet realized I needed to keep her indoors, given her non-existent attention span to what was going on around her and no desire to sit still.

When my friend Janice stopped by with her nine-year-old son, our boys went outside to play. They observed the strict instructions I'd given them to ring the doorbell before coming in. Sadly, despite their best efforts, the doorbell wasn't working, and when they walked in, Stella waltzed out. Actually, she sprinted with wild abandon, much to our horror.

Both Janice and I were in kitten heels, but that didn't stop us from jumping up to chase after Stella. Both boys followed, and all four of us were running an unintentional marathon at a complete disadvantage; four legs trump two. We were shouting, "Stella, Stella!" in the same anguished tone as Marlon Brando.

Stella raced down our small residential street, which was often referred to as a "goat road" with broken sidewalks, potholes, brush and bramble, and an occasional discarded coke can or other human trash.

Despite being in heels, we maintained our Olympic sprint after her, occasionally pole-vaulting over the obstacles in our path, given no time to think about anything beyond safe recovery of my rogue child. Taking a tumble or skinning a knee was preferred to the busy street traffic ahead of us.

Thankfully, midway down the road, Stella veered at a 90-degree angle into the local horse farm, which provided a corral for capture and safe return. I'm sure the lure of manure and all those wonderful horses in the outdoor pastures and stalls attracted her adventurous curiosity.

A competent ranch hand, whose daily chores involved managing spirited animals, lassoed her for us as we halted in place, our hearts racing and our chests heaving. We coughed through the dust cloud we'd stirred up. I wouldn't have been surprised if the wrangler had seen billows of steam coming out our ears. My relief and gratitude for his presence at that moment practically prompted me to propose marriage.

Walking Stella home, I grasped for the first time just how much responsibility was involved in caring for someone else's dog and the ingenuity required to put short-term solutions in place for the ones who lacked obedience.

The best solution for Stella's wild-child ways presented a few days later with the arrival of Otis. Otis was a Godsend of big-dog love for Stella, harmoniously matched in size and playfulness. As the two of them entertained each other, behind now-bolted doors, I was given a respite from the chase.

An important lesson to be learned here is the necessity for all pet parents to teach their dog to come when called, referred to as "recall" training. This is the most basic command in obedience training and is the most important for your dog's safety.

When indoors, most dogs stick like glue to their human companions. Many, however, will be happy to abandon their assumed guardianship role and completely reverse course when given unintentional outdoor freedom. If they escape out the door to explore, be prepared to sprint and pray for a safe return. It's easy to chase down a senior dog who simply wants to say hello to the neighbors. Any dog with Magellan verve and little recall, though, is a chase of chance.

Once your pooch is captured after the marathon event, please don't scold or punish your dog for running away. This will send the wrong message; instead, take it as a billboard moment to instigate some training using positive reinforcement methods only. Your dog may be seeking adventure due to boredom.

As dogs instinctively navigate the world by their senses, the lure of the outside world easily usurps you, as there might be more interesting sights, sounds, and smells to discover. Dogs that are kept inside with little or sporadic exercise and minimal stimulation will leap at the opportunity to create their own entertainment.

I learned my lesson with the Great Stella Chase; it's a frightening experience to pursue a loose dog. As a result, we now build the Wall of China at our entrance and exit points when our houseguests move in. We can't take the chance that, given unleashed freedom, they won't come back to us.

In all fairness, consider the hyper-charged noses on all breeds, amplified in some such as the Bloodhound, Beagle, Bassett Hound, Belgian Malinois, Coonhound, Pointer, German Shorthaired Pointer, English Springer Spaniel, German Shepherd, and Labrador, known for their superior scent abilities.

With over 220 million olfactory receptors, compared to a human's measly 5 million, a dog's nose can track and absorb the countless data found in the smells around them. It's an unfair competition between you and all that fun information out there. This is especially helpful in understanding why your dog may be reluctant to come to you yet is easily won over once you focus on this critical training assignment. Incorporate daily walks into your parenting agenda. This allows your dog to put her nose to work in a stimulating and safe way; there's the added bonus of a healthy workout for both of you.

During comprehensive recall training, consistently demonstrate the bounty she is about to receive when you call her and she complies. Coming to you, whether on command or by her own casual approach, should always result in a happy experience. Reward your dog with consistent verbal and physical praise, mixed with treats to reinforce specific behaviors you want repeated. Never use forceful or harsh punishment techniques when training your dog. I recall the caveman school of thought that swatting a dog's behind with a rolled newspaper or rubbing a puppy's nose in their own pee was "training." While it's an embarrassing admission of my age, I'm grateful to see those insidious ideas have joined the buggy whip in their usefulness.

CHAPTER FOUR

CHANGE IN LIFESTYLE WITH A DOG

As with most things in life, change doesn't happen without playful adaptation and an open mind.

Arriving home from an office meeting, in full-scale career-girl attire, I was consumed by fur and slobber. It took only one instance of being greeted by several excited dogs—my professional uniform at the mercy of their anxious fervor and toenails—to better prepare the next time.

Silk or crocheted shirts and skirts have no immunity from dogs filled with unrivaled enthusiasm and heartfelt exuberance at the mere sight of you. I learned to strip in the private sanctity of my garage and brace for the mob brawl waiting on the other side of the door.

Before I could blink, I was changing clothes as quickly as Superman and living with a revolving and diverse pack every day. I had big ones, little ones, old ones, and young ones, each with their own unique personality, coming to and going from the party in my home. Having a choir of canines also required tactical timing when I needed to speak to mortgage clients on the phone. I carefully scheduled client calls around the drop-off or pick-up of my furry guests, as a closed door was not enough to muffle the sounds echoing from a pack of barking dogs.

Every dog followed me from room to room. I felt guilty if they were resting comfortably in my home office and I needed another cup of coffee. Any movement out of the chair and down the stair prompted the pack to get up and trot to the kitchen by my side.

I side with Sally Fields who, when accepting her Best Actress award, declared to her peers: "You like me. Right now, you like me!"[2] You don't have to be an Oscar-winning actress to achieve adoration. It comes naturally to a dog who is well cared for.

The iconic actress and animal advocate Doris Day said it best: "I have found that when you are deeply troubled, there are things you get from the silent devoted companionship of a dog that you can get from no other source."[3]

Consider your lifestyle prior to dog ownership. If you have exchanged your designer duds and furnishings to suit the situation; forsaken social events or vacations when you didn't have a pet sitter you trusted; saddled up for your dog's walk when you were bone tired; risen with the sun to let them out; fallen into bed with little care about the dog hair on the sheets; and made a complete investment in their welfare with your entire heart, soul, and checkbook, then you are an official member of an elite club. If you're thinking about joining the club, first ask yourself why you want a dog and if your lifestyle will support it.

In addition to giving you their undying loyalty, dogs help you keep life's events in perspective—and provide comic relief.

2   "You like me!" Published April 21, 2011, Xavier Borderie, https://www.youtube.com/watch?v=rl_NpdAy3WY.

3   "Doris Day Quotes," Goodreads, accessed November 1, 2018, https://www.goodreads.com/author/quotes/150165.Doris_Day.

CHAPTER FIVE
WHEN TO SAY NO

Christmas is always a busy time for pet-care needs, and because I can't say no, I agreed to host twelve furry guests for the 2010 holiday. I had a foot of space left on my bed for me and slept parallel to the headboard while two Rhodesian Ridgebacks, a Weimaraner, a Shih Tzu, and my Havanese slept peacefully. There might have been an elderly poodle in the quilt somewhere too; it was a complete blur of fur.

I typically asked my clients to give me a heads-up text when they were fifteen minutes from drop-off or pick-up. This normally allowed enough time to corral my critters for a safe entrance or exit at the front door. Using portable baby gates, I would segregate the pack to minimize the cacophony and frenetic swarm at the door.

Having completely lost my wits after several days of Christmas canid escapades, I forgot to give instruction to one couple (first-time clients). When they arrived without notice and rang the doorbell, the dogs went wild.

While they waited outside patiently and anxiously for their holiday reunion with their beloved pets, I chased twelve dogs running unrestrained with vocal enthusiasm. I eventually managed to escort these wild-eyed humans through the door and into the kitchen.

We settled the bill quickly, and off they went with my best "ho ho ho!" echoing behind them. As they drove off, I discovered Mom's handbag sitting on the counter. I had to call them back for a second round of comic calamity.

As if the first embarrassing performance wasn't enough, Beau, a sweet Wheaten Terrier puppy, decided to play in a potted plant, mixing peat moss and dirt with the nearby water bowl to construct his own artistic mud creation. He spread his masterpiece all over his paws—and the floor. My clients returned to fetch the purse as I conducted an impromptu grooming moment in my bathtub.

Holding a toweled wet dog in my arms and devoid of any professional demeanor, I opened the door just a crack and shoved her personal belongings in her direction. There was no Christmas cheer left in me. Just an arm with a purse at the end of it. Not surprisingly, I never heard from them again.

Following this cuckoo Chevy Chase–like Christmas, it was more than apparent pet parents wanted what I had to offer but the business was growing bigger than me.

I had periodically encroached on my neighbor to help me manage my furry tribe. Half-crazed at times, I thrust a few dogs in her home to catch up on my sleep on an as-needed basis. My neighbors were Godsends, always waiting with a glass of wine in hand or an extra room for a short-term camper when I needed it. Still, that not-to-be-forgotten Christmas proved to be the tipping point ... sometimes there just isn't enough wine.

On the advice and encouragement of another good friend and patron, my New Year's resolution was to expand beyond the temporary pinch-hitting assistance next door and my elementary-age son and his friends. I officially began recruiting other crazy-in-love-with-dogs people to join me in sharing our homes with other people's pets.

With one hundred furry clients under my belt and several at my feet, I targeted only those who embraced my philosophy that dogs deserve to be treated like family, with constant love, affection, and attention in a cage-free boarding environment.

I focused on retirees or at-home moms and dads who weren't tied to an exterior office and could therefore dote on dogs throughout the day. Gratefully, I found them. One by one, I recruited other dog fans to augment the Doolittle's Doghouse experience.

My favorite movie as a child was the original Dr. Dolittle with Rex Harrison. If he could talk to the animals, so could we. I continued my in-home boarding while recruiting others to join the furry fray.

CHAPTER SIX

THE INITIAL CONSULTATION—SNIFFING EACH OTHER OUT

Before I would agree to board a dog, I had parents bring their charges over for a brief "yappy hour" so I could evaluate the dog's temperament and household manners. Not only did I need to visually observe the dog "in action" but also to record daily routines and determine how to best care for them *on their terms*. I thought I had this down; I knew the right questions to ask in a forty-five-minute period.

As these advance consultations rarely disqualified any dog, I prepared for the arrival of Sheila and her pup, Mona, my two Spaniels for a week. These hunting dogs belonged to a pet parent who worked in the construction business. While walking to the door with car key fob in hand, Dad casually mentioned, "Oh, by the way, the dogs are used to getting up at 3:30 a.m. 'cause that's when I leave for work."

SAY WHAT???

In for a penny, in for a pound, I prepared for sleep deprivation for the next seven days. Gratefully, Sheila and Mona allowed me to sleep in a little longer after the first night. Perhaps this change in their routine, in my favor, was a result of sleeping in the comfort of my bed as opposed to their backyard run at home. Or maybe they just felt sorry for me. I wouldn't get up at that hour to catch a flight to Europe, even if the ticket were free.

Sheila and Mona taught me the significance of a dog's individually specific routine and expectations of daily events, down to the exact hour of the day. These two were adaptable by a few hours, so I didn't have to get up every morning before the crow of a rooster.

As these early experiences prepared me to further probe pet parents for salient details, I didn't need to ask any questions when Banana arrived for her first meet and greet with me. There's something about a name.

Her dad arrived for our interview with his recently rescued German Shorthaired Pointer mix. I didn't open my mouth for the first twenty minutes; I could only watch as Banana sprinted past me through the open back door, broke the wooden slat off its shutter, ran laps in the yard, and returned to plow into a water bowl, which sent a mountainous spray onto my clothes and all over the floor. The production was followed by manic pole vaults on and off the furniture. This dog's parkour skills rivaled those of any human athlete.

As I struggled to process my thoughts, regain a sense of calm, and assess this boarding opportunity, Banana's dad mentioned that he and his partner hadn't taken a trip in the six months since Banana had come to live with them. Really, why's that?

I couldn't turn this sweet man away, so I simply asked, "When would you like to drop her off?" (I quickly followed with a subtle, yet pointed question: "And when will you be picking her up?") Banana stayed with me for three days. She settled down after the first two. I didn't have any other guests scheduled, so I did my best to be her playmate and source of entertainment 24/7.

As a single parent with a full-time job and a pet-sitting gig on the side to make ends meet, I couldn't give her the daily exercise she truly needed. The best I could do was a walk around the park. She had a need for speed. Given little time left in the day to provide it, I allowed her to use my furniture as her obstacle course. She was comfortable and content, and she was only with me for a weekend. All the love in the world isn't enough when your dog demands and deserves so much more.

The German Shorthaired Pointer is descended from various breeds going as far back as the seventeenth century. Early breeders were gunning for an all-purpose hunting dog with the versatility to track, point, and retrieve both birds and mammals. Arriving from Germany to the US in the 1920s, this breed gained recognition as the hunting dog that could do it all. Hence, if not given a daily job, with significant exercise and mental enrichment, these active breeds will become easily frustrated. They possess a great deal of energy.

I imagine Banana's original parents quickly recognized they couldn't match her liveliness, which might have been the cause for her initial surrender. Fortunately, her new owners were deeply committed to deciphering her breed coding, determined not to give up.

Banana was a one-time client for me due only to a divorce. She was kept in the family, following the requisite division of marital equity. Any dog in a custody battle should be considered an important asset to divide, along with the furniture, the house, and the vacuum cleaner.

Pet custody cases are on the rise, according to the American Academy of Matrimonial Lawyers. This is actually good news when the unfortunate and more common outcome is the dog who loses in the divorce battle and is relinquished to a shelter.

I prefer the couple who fight each other for the dog. The most outrageous example in this regard occurred between Dr. Stanley and Linda Perkins, and their dog Gigi. While joint custody was granted initially, it apparently wasn't working for either one of them. Following a two-year court battle, an estimated $150,000 in legal fees, a court-ordered bonding study by an animal behaviorist, and a videotape documenting Ms. Perkins and her interaction with Gigi, Linda was awarded sole custody.[4]

What's in the best interest of the dog after a divorce might be arguable in court. More likely, though, couples can come to a decision amicably. The best-case scenario is ultimately to keep the dog in the family. Surrender to a shelter is the worst choice and comes at the greatest expense to the dog. I'm happy that Banana was given a permanent second chance.

---

4   Christopher Mele, "When Couples Divorce, Who Gets to Keep the Dog? (Or Cat.)," *The New York Times*, March 23, 2017, https://www.nytimes.com/2017/03/23/us/divorce-pet-custody-dog-cat.html.

CHAPTER SEVEN

DOES YOUR DOG REALLY KNOW YOU?

Every move you make, every step you take, your dog is watching you! And it isn't just casual observation; it's those mega-million receptors and intuitive, associative processing skills in the span of a single moment. This data is stored in your dog's mental bank and forms his baseline of expectations and comfort in your presence. Your dog knows everything about you, and the slightest shift in your mood, movement, scent, hormones, habits, and tone of voice will not go unnoticed.

It's important to provide consistent and loving rounds of playful petting and encouraging tones of praise as often as you can. You don't want to smother your dog 24/7, yet they need the same validation of their worth that we humans do.

There are always the "can't-get-enough" attention-seeking dogs that won't let you leave the room without them or refuse to let you get back to the computer keyboard after a hug fest. I'm always careful to keep my filled-to-the-rim coffee mug on the desk in anticipation of a nose nudging my hands for more affection—especially if I'm hosting a Golden Retriever.

It's okay to say, "Enough," avert your gaze, and go about your business when your dog is begging for more attention and you're on a deadline. Sometimes it just takes a kiss on their head. It's been said that the sound of our kisses is similar to the noises a dog's birth mom makes when licking her newborn pups clean. It stands to reason that your kisses evoke a pleasurable memory and might create a quick and fond "bonding" moment between the two of you.

If kisses are pleasant sounds, loud televisions, music, shouting, fireworks and the like are not. Dogs are easily frightened by loud noises and shrieks due to their acute hearing. Many dogs suffer from "thunderstorm" anxiety due to the raucous sound of thunder or the explosion of fireworks on the Fourth of July.

A dog's hearing is measured at 45 kilohertz, while we humans tune in with 1. They can pick up high-frequency noises we never will. According to Alexandra Horowitz, author of *Inside of a Dog*, "Dogs can hear the navigational chirping of rats behind your walls and the bodily vibrations of termites within your walls."[5] She suggests that your dog is probably listening to the hum of your alarm clock and fluorescent light bulbs. This also helps explain why your dog will come running down three flights of stairs at the sound of the potato chip bag being opened.

The same sound-association phenomenon can be linked to your car in many cases. I've had some dogs playing blissfully in my walled backyard only to run to the front door when they hear their owner's car driving up the street. No advance notice or text needed. Your dog just told me you're around the corner: he knows what your car sounds like. The sound of your car is distinct to your pet, even if only subtly different from the other automobiles cruising down the same street.

Given this fresh perspective of how in tune with noises your dog is, you may want to turn down the TV and rock music and try not to yell, scream, or shout as loudly … simply drop the decibel level.

Every parent yells at their kids in a frustrated moment from time to time. Yes, we also spontaneously shriek if we see a mouse in the house or the frying pan on fire. It's those ignitable moments in life when you need to put a muzzle on your frustration because your inner pot

---

5   Alexandra Horowitz, *Inside of a Dog* (Scribner, 2010).

has boiled over. Your words, tone, and body language mean more to a dog than you think. Try to stay cool, even when your own life is heating up.

A great example of the importance of maintaining a calm demeanor, soft tones, and consistent praise and affection is best portrayed by the story of Amber and Abigail, two delightful Cocker Spaniel littermates who are regular guests of ours when their parents, Kathy and Dave, travel.

Kathy and Dave assumed guardianship following the owner's death. It was well known that the prior owner suffered from depression and would often yell at these puppies or roughly shoo them away when they approached her. Potty training was hit-and-miss, yet it was often the discovery of an accident indoors that launched a verbal tirade. The pups were isolated in the home and rarely encountered other dogs or people. They had a strong sibling bond, given the need to rely on each other for safety and comfort.

Amber and Abigail were two years old when Kathy brought them into her home. Given their isolation and inconsistent training, sporadic praise, and typical stream of invective, these two had developed an extreme fear of humans and demonstrated their insecurity by backing away and barking. Fortunately, they didn't develop biting behavior.

Kathy and her husband, Dave, spent several months showering these dogs with constant affection and ballyhoo while also providing a calmer home; they carefully controlled their personal conversations, employing softer voice tones and abundant praise. They immediately began long daily walks that included friendly encounters with strangers and dogs, to expose the girls to positive stimulation.

After months of reconditioning, they introduced Amber and Abigail to other dogs inside their new home, with careful consideration about the furry guest invitations.

Due to their patience and devotion, these two Cockers are now living happier with renewed trust of new places and faces, both human and canine.

Amber & Abigail

CHAPTER EIGHT

THE BRILLIANCE OF DOGS

Before I discovered Brian Hare's breakthrough research on a dog's cognitional abilities, I inadvertently made my own discoveries regarding their ability to understand our words, beyond voice tones.

Every dog learns what "walk" and "treat" means, as those specific words are immediately followed by joyful experiences, yet they get what we're saying in far more complex terms too.

My beloved Havanese, like any other dog with a very furry behind, was subject to a wet paper towel to remove her occasional dingleberries. It didn't take her long to figure out that when I asked, "Do you have poopy butt?" this simple grooming procedure was imminent and would send her running to hide. She associated this five-word sentence with an unpleasant violation of her privacy.

While I failed to teach her how to properly shake for a treat, she possessed enough intelligence to associate these atypical words with a specific action. I have yet to read a dog-training book that suggests "poopy butt" be used as a command to signal a grooming moment is about to follow.

Dogs have marvelous instincts to make cognitive associations, employ deductive reasoning, and apply inference from our words and actions.

My casual observations helped me understand this, yet Brian Hare, director of the Duke Canine Cognition Center at Duke University, has pioneered research that suggests dogs have a special inner "map" to successfully navigate inside our world, minds, and complex language.

His highly acclaimed book, *The Genius of Dogs*, which he co-wrote with his wife, Vanessa Woods, is based on a decade of experimental studies with outstanding results. Every dog is blessed with the innate instincts to communicate and respond via cognitive inference.

Brian Hare has proven that dogs understand what we try to convey to them in our speech. It isn't simply the intonation or clues we give, such as the excited "Wanna go for a walk?" voice we use while also grabbing our leash as a visual cue to what comes next. It's so much more than that.

Dr. Hare began his scientific journey with his childhood dog, Oreo. His father decided it would be a great idea to get Oreo to fetch the Sunday paper from their long steep driveway. Dad simply brought Oreo to the end of the driveway, pointed at the paper, and said, "Fetch paper."

When Oreo complied, he was praised. Within a week, Dad was standing at the top of the driveway, asking Oreo to "fetch paper," and Oreo knew what was wanted. Not only did this conventional dog understand the words, he got the initial gesture of pointing at the paper and applying cognitive inference as well. Other animals do not understand our pointing gestures; for example, chimpanzees don't get it. The dog has unwittingly replaced the primate in the scientific quest to better understand animals.

Dr. Hare's early observation of Oreo's abilities eventually launched a full-scale institute of meaningful and deep-rooted canine studies known as Dognition.com. In short, Hare concludes:

> We have seen that dogs are geniuses in their ability to read our gestures. Their skills are similar to what we observe in infants. The mental flexibility of dogs has led other researchers ... to suggest that dogs have a basic appreciation of our communicative intentions. They often use our behavior to infer what we want.[6]

6   Brian Hare and Vanessa Woods, *The Genius of Dogs: How Dogs Are Smarter Than You Think* (Plume, 2013).

I agree with Dr. Hare and have personally witnessed all dogs' abilities to understand our communication, intentions, body language, spoken words, and inner emotions. They sense by their unique canine instincts of comprehensive interpretation. Dr. Hare further states:

> Relative to other animals, it is the ability of dogs to understand human communication that is truly remarkable. Some dogs have the ability to learn hundreds of names for objects. They learn these names extremely rapidly, through an inferential process of exclusion. They also spontaneously understand the category to which different objects belong. Some dogs even show understanding of the symbolic nature of human object labels. Dogs may truly understand words.[7]

Beyond simple commands for obedience, dogs interpret our whole language and specifically targeted words and sentences, as evidenced by the infamous Border Collie "Chaser".

Chaser's dad, Dr. John W. Pilley, was a renowned Wofford College professor and psychologist who adopted her as a young puppy. In three years' time, Chaser was taught to recognize over one thousand different objects, including toys, balls, and Frisbees, each by its individual name. Combining different objects of various sizes and categories, with a name for each, Dr. Pilley taught Chaser to identify each one with remarkable accuracy.

While many of us have neither PhD credentials nor the time to elevate our dog's skills to Chaser's level, any dog will quickly recognize the difference between categories of objects such as high heels and tennis shoes.

Puppies, of course, haven't developed discrimination of objects yet and will gladly munch on anything without discernment, probably

---

7   Hare and Woods, *The Genius of Dogs.*

starting with the most expensive footwear. Let's call those the Jimmy Chews.

As your dog constantly observes and learns from you, she will quickly associate objects with meaning. When your high heels, purse, and keys come out, this typically means you are leaving the house without her.

She understands that tennis shoes, however, often signal a walk. This simple wardrobe change can send your dog jumping for joy, *before* you grab the leash. I've experienced that "oh boy" excitement following the benign appearance of a pair of athletic socks, the precedent to running shoes.

Apart from object inference, specific hand signals used by professional trainers are universal cues for dogs. You've probably worked with these various techniques, similar to a street cop directing traffic with body and hand motions.

When I have a dog's attention, holding their gaze, I extend a palm up and flick my fingers to non-verbally communicate "come here." It's an easy signal to interpret and typically met with their approach. It can also work without the flick … just an open palm. Simply patting the empty seat next to you can prompt a leap beside your lap.

If a dog is barking for no reason, I use one hand, create an L with the index finger and thumb, and firmly state "quiet." I am not smiling when I do this, yet not employing a "mad" face either. I picked this up from Cesar Milan with periodic success. The L, serious face, and one word. It will get their attention at that moment as they try to interpret what your unique hand formation is conveying. "Good quiet" and a treat, if handy, should follow this temporary halt so they understand your signaled intention. I cannot guarantee that the barking will stop. Chronic barking is a training issue and best left to a professional.

I *can* guarantee that frequently smiling at your dog will promote greater reassurance and happiness than an angry face will. A report by *Frontiers in Behavioral Neuroscience* describes results proving a dog's ability to discriminate between neutral and happy facial expressions.[8] Dogs excel at reading social and facial cues.

As our goal is to promote a tail-wagging experience, we kick off every stay with a happy face in a fun, quiet, and cheery place. I know the feelings are mutual; the release of oxytocin, our "love" hormone, has been proven to occur between humans and their furry best friends.

A celebrated study supporting this idea was conducted by Takefumi Kikusui, an animal behaviorist at the Azabu University in Sagamihara, Japan. Kikusui gathered thirty dogs and their owners into his lab to interact for thirty minutes with petting, talking, and short intervals of eye-gazing moments.

Using before and after urine samples from all subjects, he found that in the pairs who gazed at each other longer, the oxytocin levels in the humans spiked by 300% and the levels in the dogs increased by 130%. If you've felt the same heart-flipping emotion when gazing into your dog's eyes, you now have the science to back up this cause-and-effect event.

For a fun study you can try at home to analyze how your dog thinks and feels, I'll point you in the direction of Brian Hare's science-based games designed to measure five core dimensions of a dog's behavioral and emotional skills: Empathy, Communication, Cunning, Memory, and Reasoning.

---

8   Anna Kis, Anna Hernádi, Bernadett Miklósi, Orsolya Kanizsár, and József Topál, "The Way Dogs (*Canis familiaris*) Look at Human Emotional Faces is Modulated by Oxytocin," *Front. Behav. Neurosci.*, October 31, 2017, https://doi.org/10.3389/fnbeh.2017.00210.

His innovative Dognition Assessment program was developed by a team of specialists in the field of dog behavior and training. Following online instruction, with specific interactive games to play with your dog, you will be able to determine your dog's unique character within Hare's creative spectrum of nine personality profiles. Is your dog an Ace, Charmer, Socialite, Expert, Renaissance, Protodog, Einstein, Stargazer, or Maverick?

The ubiquity of dogs and the similarity of their physiology to our own are fascinating not only to scientists but also to the individual owner who instinctively believes that their dog is human.

CHAPTER NINE
FOOD GLORIOUS FOOD

One particular human-like tendency in dogs is noncompliance at chow time. Feeding multiple dogs that don't normally live together can be a hoot as not every dog is interested in their food, particularly when they get a whiff of something new and different. I appreciate the Labs, Beagles, Pugs, and similar breeds with greedy guts; they gobble their kibble regardless of the brand or how long they've been served the same daily menu without diversity.

My pet nannies have experienced the same disregard for meals with many of their guests as well. Frequent conversations ensue as to how best to get their guest to eat, short of performing circus tricks, standing on their heads, or feeding them by hand.

Not only are we rearranging the furniture and dividing our houses to create separate "dining" rooms, we have collectively experienced that not every dog eats their food with gusto.

It is gastronomically obvious to us that some dogs are simply bored with their diet. Parents might drop them off with the caveat: "He's a picky eater." Yes, some dogs are chronically picky eaters. Just like human children, they may not want to eat their vegetables.

However, the majority of the time, we add a little grated cheese, chicken broth, or a tiny bit of chicken or salmon to encourage consumption (unless given strict instructions regarding a guest's dietary restrictions).

In many cases, our guests have never seen a change in their menu, and the same food eaten every day has lost its flavor. Some dog food simply lacks flavor out of the bag.

While I was raised eating squirrel and rabbit, and our dogs ate whatever crappy kibble my dad bought or shot, I have since learned that good-quality nutrition is as important to them as it is to us.

My first dog as an adult was Max, a beloved Leonberger I will always cherish in my heart. This is not a breed you see every day. It originated in Leonberg, Germany, where its creator, Heinrich Essig, lived. Essig mated the Newfoundland, Great Pyrenees, and Saint Bernard in order to achieve a leonine look. The goal was to duplicate the lion in the town crest of Leonberg, Germany, in a dog. Somehow, Heinrich managed to eliminate the drooling of the Bernard.

Leonbergers are rare in many regards. While originally bred for aesthetics, this dog has grown to embody incredible intelligence and gentleness, and the heart of a lion. Breed books praise this dog as a great addition to a family, as they will tolerate a toddler's poking and prodding—even pencils stuck up the nose—without flinching.

Our local vet at the time, Dr. Richard Soltero Sr., was an early pioneer for the virtues of a raw meat diet for dogs and cats. He also told me that "people food was okay," with obvious exceptions, of course. Max became my compliant garbage disposal. Having grown up in Iowa, a cattle-producing state, I love a good grilled steak, and Max did too.

I enjoyed sharing low-fat table scraps with Max but did not embrace feeding him a raw diet, nor did I explore other higher-quality dry food alternatives. I did not pay attention to the ingredients in the big-box-store kibble we served daily as his main meal. It was undoubtedly chock-full of preservatives and synthetic ingredients designed to last longer on the grocery store shelf. But I didn't know any better then. Max succumbed to cancer at the age of eleven.

I thought I was doing everything right at the time. Max went to puppy obedience classes and, like a good student, learned to be polite, play well with others, and follow the curriculum that would promote good canine citizenship.

He was loveable and had good manners. As he matured, I took him everywhere with me; he even attended client loan application appointments. We would pull up in our convertible, looking like a *Marmaduke* cartoon, and Max would accompany me as I analyzed the clients' financial wherewithal. Max unwittingly provided emotional therapy to those who may have been nervous about their mortgage qualifications.

When I vacationed without him, he was boarded in the home of a local Leonberger breeder. Roz lived on a quasi-farm with her own Leos, at least three at a time when she didn't have a litter of them. I drove one hour each way to give Max this special cage-free boarding experience with his "cousins." While I resented the long-distance sojourn it required, it was worth it to provide Max a vacation oasis of his own. This was my first introduction to the concept of cage-less boarding in a private home, yet it would be many years before I duplicated the concept myself.

Max and Me

If I'd known then what I know now about the importance of quality cuisine, Max and I might have had more time together. I surely would have invested in higher-grade grains and proteins and also scheduled more frequent well exams with our vet instead of waiting for routine vaccination appointments or taking him in when something unusual popped up.

When Max was an adolescent, he developed bumps on his nose. A quick, panic-stricken trip to the vet revealed they were pimples. My vet simply used his fingers to squeeze the offensive zits, and off we went with a smooth snout. Who would think a dog could develop acne?

As dogs enter their golden years, it is prudent to get a *semiannual* checkup with all the "groceries," such as blood work and X-rays. This will help flush out any underlying conditions that can be successfully treated if caught early.

I'm grateful for the eleven years we had together. The Leonberger breed is not expected to live longer than an estimated nine years. But what determines the life span of each dog? Larger dogs live shorter lives, perhaps due to their accelerated growth as puppies and the more-rapid development of age-related illnesses later. Working dogs tend to live longer as they maintain a healthier weight while keeping physically fit. Obesity is a huge problem with all dogs and has a definite and undesired impact on their long-term health.

If breed-book statistics are based on "averages," is it because the "average dog" isn't getting a proper diet with seasonal adjustments as needed, proper and regular exercise, and daily mental enrichment? While many variables will determine your dog's longevity, a balanced and nutritionally rich diet is the most important ingredient for their health and vitality.

For most dog owners, food choice and vet visits boil down to cost. To maintain a manageable budget, many owners tend to visit the family veterinarian only when a medical condition surfaces or when the vaccination reminder arrives in the mail.

When comparing the price of dog food, the bigger, cheaper bag of kibble may seem to be the financially logical choice, yet it may not be the best health plan for your dog.

Although dogs are officially classified as omnivores, protein is the most important ingredient for them. In the wild, a canine's diet is 80% meat. Take a peek at the ingredients in your dog's food. In conjunction with what you're putting down for his meals, please also consider appropriate *life-stage* nutritional needs.

Many veterinarians will agree the best diet for dogs should include a combination of quality ingredients, focusing on the same four main food groups we were schooled on: protein, fresh fruits and vegetables, carbohydrates, and essential supplements and vitamins.

Grass-fed meat is higher in nutritional value and a better choice than feedlot meat. Range-free chicken, lamb, and eggs are best, along with wild fish.

For the picky eaters, rotational feeding may be appropriate. You might need to experiment with different foods to find the right balance of nutrition, taste, and daily amount.

If your dog is simply bored with his daily diet, providing variety may help. I learned this while observing my pack—especially those who wanted what the other dogs were eating. When dining with friends or family, do you ask for a small bite of their meals or announce to the waitress, "I'll have what they're having"? Similarly, would you order the same meal every day without wavering as your own dietary needs change over time?

Some dogs just naturally stage a hunger strike, despite their owner's best efforts. If you have a dog who has sampled every brand known to man and continues to ignore his food, consider a food puzzle as a last-ditch twist. Fun and entertaining, a puzzle to be solved in order to find the hidden grub may provide the mental exercise and effort needed to stimulate his appetite.

Dogs eat less in the summer months, so don't confuse reduced consumption with the natural metabolic changes that occur seasonally. We tend to exercise them less in extreme weather conditions, which logically results in a reduced desire for food.

No dog will starve themselves, unless they are really sick. An otherwise healthy dog will "hold their nose" and eventually eat what you have made available, notwithstanding the food hounds that gulp anything out of simple gratitude or breed nuance.

It's emotionally challenging as a canine caregiver to glance into the eyes of those that stare at their food bowl and look up as if to say, "Is this all you've got?"

I highly recommend Dr. Richard Soltero's book, *It's Like a Miracle*, not only for the endearing stories about his vast veterinary experiences, but also for his personal journey that led to astounding research and conclusions about the striking correlation between canine cancer and diet.

Dr. Soltero advocates raw diets for pets. His clinic was peppered with photos of dogs and cats both before and after a dietary change to raw food. The transformations rival any supermodel arriving on a shoot before makeup. He proudly displayed the images of skinny, sickly, and semi-hairless dogs and cats before being fed a raw diet; then in as little as six weeks, like cocooned butterflies breaking free, these animals demonstrated an astounding metamorphosis. Dr. Soltero's personal and professional superfood quest led to the publishing of his book in 2007, at a time when canine cancer research was in its infancy.

According to the National Canine Cancer Foundation, one out of three dogs will be diagnosed with cancer. The foundation is committed to education, outreach, and research to benefit dog owners who may face this serious disease at some point in their dog's life.

As an Arizona State University graduate, I am immensely impressed with my alma mater and the fieldwork applications within their Canine Science Collaboratory department.

The Open Philanthropy Project, an independent organization that identifies research opportunities, has recently granted $6.4 million to the ASU Biodesign Institute to test a vaccine for canine cancer. The specific vaccine, a "multivalent frameshift peptide (FSP)"—whatever that means to us laypeople—was actually created ten years ago by Stephen Albert Johnston.

This grant will help promote the largest canine clinical trial with close to 800 dogs enrolled in the study. In collaboration with several scientists and other cancer institutes, this will be a five-year project, injected with lots of hope for the future.

As these brilliant biologists work toward a future vaccination, it is imperative that the rest of us focus on the ingredients in our dog's food as a possible contributor to canine cancer. This assumes we can actually decipher what's listed on those labels; they might as well be written in Greek.

In addition to Dr. Soltero's early and startling observations, other renowned veterinarians are taking a closer look at what's causing this alarming rise in pet cancer, starting with processed dog food.

A favorite houseguest always arrived with the same rainbow-colored kibble and, after one sniff, gave me *the look*. I had read about the public controversy regarding the other 3,000 dogs eating the same stuff and getting sick. While I'm not in a position to arbitrarily change any dog's diet or refuse to put out what's been provided, at a minimum I can drop a hint about the nutrient-deficient kibble in their tote bag and hope pet parents take the bait.

I fondly remember one guest who was on a raw meat diet and loved it most when served only partially thawed. A 16-x-4 inch, 10-pound slab of frozen meat landed in my freezer upon Leroy's arrival. Leroy was a healthy, stout Lab who had the jaws for meat with ice still on it.

I pulled out my electric carving knife to portion off each meal twice a day and store it in the refrigerator for only twenty-four hours. While it was a workout to cut through this brick, I knew it was a great food choice this dog's dad was making for his furry son; and my dusty kitchen utensil, reserved for the non-existent Thanksgiving turkey, was finally put to good use.

Kaia and Kismet, two American Eskimos, are show-breed dogs. The American Eskimo Dog originally descended from the German Spitz, which became a favorite of circus performers in the 1920s. Following World War I, the name was changed to American Eskimo. It should come as no surprise that they love cold weather. The two of them are absolute clowns and a joy to have around.

We first met this family when Kaia was about to come into heat. As Kismet is intact, they needed to be safely separated—by miles—so Kismet was to board with us until Kaia's "season" passed.

Following the initial consultation with Kelly, Kathy, Kismet, and my nannies Jeri and Mike, we waited until nature kicked in. Kismet was promptly whisked away for several weeks and returned home when the coast was clear. Kismet had a ball with Jeri and Mike, including lake outings on their boat, while Kelly and Kathy kept Kaia at home under lock and key.

She is now spayed. Once was apparently enough for these owners! Showing and breeding are two disparate endeavors; the former was the road more easily traveled for this special family of "Eskie" lovers.

Their diet is an assemblage of organic foods, which include cooked skinless chicken, frozen vegetables of all varieties, My Perfect Pet (frozen) Low Glycemic Turkey (made with fresh whole foods turkey, yam, green beans, broccoli, and kale) and Low Glycemic Chicken (made with fresh whole foods chicken, green beans, broccoli, zucchini, yams, celery, cranberries, kale and collards), and two varieties of Blue Buffalo canned wet food containing a laundry list of superior ingredients.

Noticeably absent is a large amount of output in the backyard. The higher the quality of food going into your dog, the smaller the size of their stools. Double bonus to good dog nutrition!

Their portmanteau is also packed with an electronic scale to measure different portions of chicken for each dog's size and weight, cheese sticks split and served daily at 11:00 a.m., Schwan's frozen doggie sundaes for periodic treats, and finally, pure pumpkin *just in case.*

There's a lot of hair back there, and a loose stool necessitates some serious bath time, in addition to the routine brushing and grooming necessary for this breed.

I wholly embrace the natural benefits of pure pumpkin, not only as a dietary supplement but also for its fibrous, stool-firming properties. It can work in the reverse too—when your dog is constipated and needs help launching a movement.

Every dog will develop short-term diarrhea, yet in most cases, a small dollop of pure pumpkin added to each meal will typically achieve Tootsie-Roll normalcy within twenty-four hours. It's sold on grocery store shelves and in boutique pet stores that carry organic versions. Note: pure pumpkin is not the same as pumpkin pie filling. Go pure for sure. I can confidently recommend this simple home remedy; at the first sign things aren't working out right, go for the pure pumpkin.

While some veterinarians will prescribe Pepto-Bismol, a short-term diet change to white rice and chicken, or pills to cure the diarrhea ills, I personally prefer this quick and easy alternative. I've witnessed its fast and remarkable results 90% of the time.

If your dog's diarrhea persists longer than twenty-four hours, is accompanied by vomiting and/or lethargy, or turns to soupy liquid, rush to your vet as this is more than normal tummy upset.

Kaia and Kismet's daily restaurant-quality meal preparation could be an episode for Rachel Ray's audience. These are undoubtedly two of the healthiest dogs in our ring, with super-sweet dispositions, easygoing manners, and an abundance of affection. As they are on the professional road often, their resilience and adaptability to new surroundings shows. Not one whimper or ounce of anxiety.

Kelly and Kathy are pet parents with panache; they have committed their livelihood to the health and vitality of their dogs, and they give their time, effort, and expense to showcase this unique breed across the country.

Kelly will tell you that in order to become a millionaire showing dogs professionally, you have to be a multimillionaire before you start! One show in particular involved an RV rental and, all told, the expenses amounted to a $10,000 performance. The UKC (United Kennel Club) offers an "altered" division for those dogs who have been spayed or neutered. AKC confirmations require intact status.

All of this fanfare is for the prize of "Best in Show," for which ribbons are awarded. These are expensive ribbons that reflect the breed dedication of those who travel the country to exhibit their champions.

Kaia & Kismet-the "Eskie" family

CHAPTER TEN

CANINE AND FELINE CANCER

For a real taste of the importance of quality dog food for your pets, consider a cursory review of the electric documentary *The Truth About Pet Cancer* in the interest of awareness and education only. Many industry specialists have come to the table to espouse their opinions regarding the environmental and dietary elements that may be leading causes of pet cancer, which has reached epidemic proportions.

Not all veterinary practitioners will agree with the information shared in this documentary. There will always be a right-to-left debate between conventional practice and emerging non-conventional interests incorporating a more holistic approach to the care of our dogs and cats. Perhaps there's a reasonable middle ground to be found where "East meets West."

The information contained in this well-versed series of professional *dialogues* is shocking and a *cause to paws* and reevaluate your approach to your dog's dietary health. Ty Bollinger is the producer of this documentary. The individuals he has interviewed are an impressive and interesting coalition of veterinarians, biologists, professors, and food scientists. While the information may be controversial, there's considerable common sense to be read between the lines.

Janice, my good friend and long-distance runner mentioned earlier, has a dog who suffers from chronic GI issues. On a mission to help her dog from the inside out, Janice began by consulting her veterinarian about a new diet as the logical starting point. Her corporate-salaried veterinarian told her that other pet foods not sold on their shelf could neither be discussed nor recommended.

Food for thought, as the actual processing of some pet foods in America might make your stomach turn if you care to learn more.

Integrative vet medicine, combining conventional wisdom with alternative treatments and prevention, is the thrust behind Ty Bollinger's *The Truth About Pet Cancer.* Take it with a grain of non-GMO salt.

The following is an excerpt of dialogue from Episodes 1 and 2, related to pet food:

Dr. Judy Morgan, DVM, CVA, CVCP, CVFT, Holistic Veterinarian of 33+ years:

> Back in the fifties, we had farm dogs, and they ate what was left over from what was grown on the farm, and we weren't using such horrible chemicals on the plants and the crops. And we weren't feeding processed food to our animals. They were eating whole, nutritious, real foods.

Ty Bollinger:

> In every war, there are casualties. Rather than fight cancer, why not educate everyone about cancer's true causes and treatments, especially in our pet? One area where I believe we all could use some education is learning how to decipher exactly what the ingredients are in pet food.

Dr. Peter Dobias, DVM, Holistic Veterinarian:

> And if you look at their labels, it blows my mind that these foods are used. There's modified starch, and corn, and meat byproducts, and rendered fat, and whatever else is actually not part of the natural diet of our canines or felines, or other animals.

Lori Taylor, CEO & Founder of TruPet:

[Animals are] not smoking cigarettes, they're not drinking, they're not doing some of the things that you and I do that help create an environment that's super available for cancer. They're not stressed out in their minds ... And so, what is it? To me, what landed for me at that time ... was that it had to be something that we are feeding them. So, I started to look on the back of the label to figure it out. And then as I started reading the label, I was like *I don't even know what 90% of this is*.

Dr. Judy Morgan:

No. I mean what you're taught in school is to never let your clients do a home-cooked meal. Do not let them feed anything from the table. Oh my gosh, God forbid. If they feed scraps from the table, they will unbalance the balanced diet that they're pouring with the kibble into the bowl. What a bunch of malarkey.

Dr. Karen Becker, DVM, Holistic Veterinarian and author of *Real Food for Healthy Dogs and Cats*:

When it comes to nutrition, there's a lot of issues in the pet food industry that we're up against. And I believe that how we choose to nourish our animals on a day-to-day basis absolutely impacts their immunologic health.

Ty Bollinger:

Does your vet recommend kibble? If so, do they tell you that in 2014, three of the biggest pet food manufacturers were found to have aflatoxins in their pet food? Now, aflatoxins are known to be carcinogens ... in 2015, one of the largest pet food manufacturers was found to have mycotoxins, which are fungal toxins, in their food, as well as different bacteria that the FDA determined to be qualifying pathogens and that they posed a serious threat to public health … The sad thing is that pet parents just do not know … If the cancer-causing agent is added to the carcasses before arriving at the pet food manufacturing plant, then it does not have to be included on the label.

Just to be clear, ethoxyquin is commonly found in many popular brands of pet food, and it's been linked to canine liver and kidney cancer. Other ingredients to look out for are BHA, which has been linked to tumors and liver failure, and BHT, which is another preservative linked to cancer and endocrine disruption.

Dr. Judy Morgan:

So, I mean back in 2006, we had the melamine toxicity that killed tens of thousands of pets with kidney disease, because that was added overseas in China. Nobody bothered to test it. And the wheat gluten. We have propylene glycol as a preservative. We have tons of sugar. We have tons of salt. They're used as preservatives. We have red dyes. But a dog doesn't care if it's dyed green, yellow, purple, and red. That's all for the consumer.

And the pet food companies are spending a lot more money on advertising, the big ones, than they are on ingredients. And so, when we go to these meetings, there are industry representatives in there from the waste oil industry, and from the grocery waste industry, and they're just trying to figure out how to sell their waste products to pet food companies.

Dr. Judy Morgan:

So, they can get paid for all their waste products. So, recycled restaurant oils. It doesn't go into dog food, but it goes into cattle feed … all those expired dairy products, all those expired bakery products, go out in the dumpster, sit in the sun for a while, then they get picked up and they go to a plant and they get all mashed together and ground up, and then it goes into cattle feed … We're feeding it to the cows. Well, do you think it comes out in the milk and the meat?

Ty Bollinger:

We really have to start looking around and going "How did nature do it?" And then "Can we mimic what nature does?" If we mimicked what nature does, we'd follow what dogs and cats eat in the wild.

Mike "Health Ranger" Adams, Food Scientist and Founder of Naturalnews.com:

You don't see wild dogs chewing on corn and wheat and grain. They are hunting other animals, coyotes and wolves. And that gives you a clue about the proper nutritional balance of your own dog, because your dog is not a vegetarian.

Dr. Will Falconer, DVM, Certified Veterinarian Homeopath at Vital Animal:

Dogs and wolves are like this for DNA—99% match, if you look at what's called the mitochondrial DNA. So, what does a wolf eat in the wild? They eat prey; it's always fresh and it's alive and it's raw and it's balanced. They don't just eat the muscles and run off. They eat bone, they eat the organs, they eat a little bit of digested vegetation that's been semi-digested. We can do things like that at home, but this bag of kibble is nothing like it. It's dead, it's full of toxic ingredients, and genetically speaking the dog is saying, "Hey, you domesticated me and I'm cute and all, but digestively I still got that call within saying 'Where is prey?'"

Dr. Thomas N. Seyfried, PhD, Professor of Biology, Boston College:

The whole thing is convenience. You come home, you're working all day long. The dog is so happy to see you, he's all excited. You throw the food into the bowl, the dog is just really happy, wolfs it down. Literally, wolfs it down, and eats the same thing every day. You don't give him a variety. You come home and eat the same thing every day, you'll say "What the hell is going on here, why am I getting the same thing every day?"

Dogs did not evolve to eat the same thing every day either, so the whole thing is upside down...They're getting all kinds of the same kinds of problems that we have as a species; they are suffering from the same kind of maladies that we suffer from. And do you think there might be a common link in what they're eating?

Lori Taylor:

Because on a dog food label, they do rank them from how much is actually weighted in the bag, from number one to zero, to the last ingredient. And when you look at that first ingredient, you know how people are like, "Oh, our first ingredient's chicken." And then maybe you'll see that second ingredient's usually byproduct or chicken meal.

Ty Bollinger:

Could it be that kibble is actually part of our unknowing contribution to this manmade disease we call cancer?

Dr. Will Falconer:

The common word is *byproducts*. What does that mean? Well byproducts can include, and often does, the 4D meats. I don't know if you've run into the term, but 4D stands for dead, diseased, dying, or disabled cows when they come to slaughter, or pigs or whatever. So that can't go to human consumption, but boy, the pet food manufacturers snap that up. It's a bargain; it's protein.

Dr. Karen Becker:

> To manufacture high-quality, human-grade, excellent-quality meat-based pet food is incredibly expensive. So, 100 years ago the pet food industry substituted excellent-quality protein for rendered protein, which is really how we recycle the leftover pieces and parts from the human food industry. It goes into pet food. And then we use a lot of unnatural fillers. Corn, wheat, rice, soybeans, now we're using grain-free options like a lot of potato, a lot of lentil, a lot of tapioca, a lot of starch, because meat is expensive... So, pet foods are really constituted of a lot of high-carbohydrate, high-glycemic index foods along with some rendered protein and a synthetic multivitamin.

What we might conclude from the above dialogue excerpts is the reality that preservatives in pet food are designed to extend product shelf life, yet BHT and BHA are toxic and carcinogenic.

Fillers in pet food, such as barley, oatmeal, soy, corn, and wheat lack significant nutritional value. And slaughterhouse waste and meat byproducts are nasty ingredients that are being fed to unsuspecting consumers and their pets, *in some pet food products.*

The Truth about Pet Cancer is a 7-part docu-series, which also includes further debate on the following topics: vaccines and parasite prevention products, other pet cancer causes, cancer roots and remedies, and treatment and prevention.

It's important to note that not all pet food manufacturers should be lumped into a pervasive category of "profit-motivated only" designers of dog food. There are many companies that diligently oversee plant processing protocols and ingredient resources to provide superior-quality food for dogs and cats.

A complete and unbiased list of current dog food manufacturers and brand-name products was reviewed by a team of non-industry analysts at Reviews.com and provided by Jacqueline Ma for our website. Their evaluations are extremely detailed and also outline the parameters used to measure their "top picks" and those that didn't make the grade. I encourage your consumption of this article https://doolittlesdoghouse.com/the-best-dog-food-by-reviews-com/ to assist you in your quest to find the best food for your dog.

If you are what you eat, the same adage applies to your dog. What's in your dog's food bowl?

CHAPTER ELEVEN
RESCUE GROUPS, SHELTERS, AND FOSTER FAMILIES—SUPERHEROES

I admire animal rescue groups, shelters, support volunteers, and foster families engaged in significant efforts to rescue, rehabilitate, and rehome abandoned and abused dogs and cats.

As most animal rescue organizations operate independently, especially the breed-specific groups with limited resources, one particularly impressive coalition in Arizona, the Phoenix Animal Care Coalition, aka PACC911, demonstrates the prodigious success that can be achieved by unified effort.

Founded by Bari Mears in 1999, PACC911 combines over 100 animal welfare organizations in a unique and well-structured alliance. This brilliant collaboration provides fundraising events, education forums, a food bank to assist low-income families with food for their pets, and medical aid to help ill or injured animals. They also regularly host mega adopt-a-thons.

The latter events are held monthly in large outdoor venues for their rescue partner members to showcase adoptable pets. With the coalition's commitment to presenting hundreds of healthy, adoptable dogs and cats in an outdoor setting, hopeful pet owners can experience a more enjoyable and stress-free landscape as they search for a new companion. This escape-the-shelter environment has helped unite over 10,000 animals with new families, and renewed hope for happiness.

A Glimmer of Hope

Read the news most any day, dismal stories fill the page
On TV there is no end to human cruelty, greed and rage.
But today when least expected almost at my end of rope
I was touched by human kindness, witnessing a ray of hope.

A little one abandoned when the family moved away
Left without a morsel and was told to sit and stay.
As days went by his hunger was coupled by his fear
So starved for food and company, he longed for kindness to appear.

Whimpering he cried for help, then howled a piercing wail
Unanswered were his mournful pleas, and all to no avail.
Though many ears did hear his calls, they were deafened to the sound
Too self-absorbed to listen, unconcerned to come around.

Then in the quiet of a dark, cold night, one tired "woof" was heard
Soon open arms embraced him with a soothing, caring word.
Angels grace the heavens, touching down to help the meek
On earth we call them rescuers, no glory do they seek.

They'll travel from the mountaintops or traverse a slippery slope
To save a pup or kitties life …. A glimmer now, of hope.
They are angels wearing tennis shoes, worn blue jeans and a tee
They give voice to those who cannot speak, and hope for humanity.[9]

9   Bari Mears, "A Glimmer of Hope," *Pawprints on the Heart* (PACC911 Publications, 2009).

Missy's story is an ideal example of how this prodigious group united a darling dog with the right owner, a tale of hope and promise brought to life through the power of rescue groups.

Enjoying afternoon tea with friends, Ann announced that she wanted to adopt a dog, although she had planned a month-long vacation so she had to postpone her companionship pursuit for nine months. As I dogged the PACC911's activities, I knew there was a two-day mega adoption event occurring that weekend.

I encouraged Ann to attend and offered to host (at no cost) any dog she came home with. The next day, which was the last day of the event, Ann spent several hours visiting each rescue group's booth yet didn't make a connection. As the affair was winding down and volunteers began packing their tents and crating up the shelter pets that hadn't found a home, Ann also prepared to leave … alone. As Ann arrived at the exit gate, in the last booth by the parking lot, Missy pirouetted just in time to catch Ann's eye. Something about this adorable Chi-weenie mix captured her heart, and Ann found a passenger for life.

Not only did I maintain my commitment to care for Missy while Ann traveled later that summer, Missy has fulfilled every promise to provide uplifting companionship for Ann. Missy, aka Sassy Pants, is a crowd pleaser in every way. It's easy to tell when Missy is happy, which is particularly noticeable if she is the only dog in the room. She loves to be the center of attention, and she shimmies like a baton-twirler while looking right at you with a gleam in her big brown eyes that says, "Aren't I cute?" She prances on her front paws, one at a time, like a Lipizzaner in a dressage performance. She's also one of those dogs that whirls and twirls in complete circles when she's happy and wants to convey her cuteness—or is expecting a baby carrot for her treat. In anticipation of a meal, as her bowl is prepared, this tiny trencherman will leave the ground, jumping up and down—often on her hind legs only. Missy is a petite, black and brown bundle of love that completes Ann's life. Ann is a single gal with many friends, yet none is more devoted to her than Missy.

There are way too many parade cheerleaders like Missy waiting for permanent homes and the chance to unleash their full potential.

Missy - the Cheerleader

In addition to PACC911's collective efforts, another unique program I would love to see adopted by animal shelters is the "Take a Dog for a Day." Given the shortage of available foster families, and too many overcrowded shelters with overly stressed dogs, Aspen Animal Shelter nails it with a very loose, open-to-the-public program that allows any responsible adult to stop by the shelter and "check out" a dog for the day.

When on holiday, I noticed many of their parolees, identified by company vests, cruising around the outdoor pedestrian malls and parks. A quick survey of the tourists who were walking these dogs led me to the shelter the next day to retrieve one of my own. I was cheerfully greeted by a staff member, signed in with no more than a copy of my driver's license, and escorted to the play yard where a few, pre-screened dogs were introduced to me one by one. I chose Shiloh, a skinny non-descript Shepherd mix with a skittish personality and resigned passivity.

While I was advised that she might not want to stray too far from "home," as the shelter had been her only refuge for two years, we had a lovely afternoon together, walking in a greenbelt area nearby. She seemed thrilled at the opportunity to feel grass on her feet, experience new sights and smells, and stretch her legs.

Having lost my own dog recently and still grieving, I found the entire experience immensely rewarding and undoubtedly got more out of this short-lived moment of reprieve than she did. Her energy didn't wane when it was time to head back, much like a pack mule who knows only one road.

As I prepared to leave the Aspen Animal Shelter, I bumped into the still-handsome, now-retired actor Robert Wagner, a fierce advocate and supporter of this privatized, non-profit no-kill sanctuary. How cool was that for this star-struck hick chick? More importantly, how hard is it to unlock the cage and allow a shelter pet a pardon for the day?

Seth Sachson is the proverbial Oz behind the curtain of this magnificent shelter operation, with real and meaningful dedication to his canine village. They house 20–30 shelter dogs at any one time, offer boarding and grooming for town locals, and keep the doors open 365 days a year.

Seth launched this unique "exercise your heart, exercise a dog" program twenty-five years ago. While many shelters shy away from the potential liability and risk, Seth perseveres because, as he states, "the good outweighs the bad."

Confident in his ability to selectively match the human walker with the right dog, he provides a much-needed, short escape for the dog. Even better, many of the dogs are adopted by the same tourist or town resident.

He is careful to redirect the suspicious volunteers with artful diversion, including the occasional individual with the right idea but wrong day, showing up late in the afternoon with alcohol on their breath.

I'm flattered that I was given such a quick pass in the screening process. I must have shown that I wasn't an idiot who would think to let a dog I didn't know run off leash or allow her to get nose to nose with another unknown dog while we were walking in the park. Our brief meet and greet in their outdoor shelter yard was sufficient evidence that the dog and I could soberly trot off together without incident, accident, or injury to either of us.

To emphasize the huge benefit for these lost-my-home innocents, Lisa Gunter, psychology doctoral candidate at the ASU Canine Science Collaboratory, proffers three studies focusing on the welfare of shelter dogs.

The first study involved "sleepovers" where dogs from a specifically targeted shelter spent a night away with a foster parent. Cortisol levels were measured at the shelter before departure, during their overnight away, and upon return. Just one night away led to significant reductions in stress hormones. Taking it one step further, Lisa and her team expanded the study to include dogs from four different shelters in various cities. For the second study, the dogs spent *two* nights with a foster parent, with the same measurement protocols.

The concern was that cortisol levels might be higher if the dogs had a two-day vacation (versus one) followed by their return to the shelter with bigger disappointment or shock, the longer they were away. Interestingly enough, Lisa and her team found that a two-day vacation tested the same as the one-day, and at *all four shelters*—every furloughed dog showed reduction in cortisol levels.

According to Gunter: "Our interpretation is that these sleepovers are kind of like a weekend to the workweek … it doesn't make all the dogs' stress go away but it lets them go to a house, take a breather, rest and recharge. And then come back to the shelter ready to find their forever home."[10]

I agree with Lisa Gunter and her studied team of scientists: "The fact that we saw the sleepover intervention working... suggests to us that it would be a useful practice [for shelters to implement]."[11]

I encourage every rescue group, shelter, spirited and innovative leaders, and volunteers to copy the coalition model of PACC911 and consider short-term "vacation" programs like the one Aspen Animal Shelter offers, which has been proven to have positive benefits for prisoners on four paws.

Working in charitable concert can create a louder voice on behalf of those animals left behind without a choice.

---

10   Emma Greguska, "Giving pound puppies a paw up," ASU Now, April 11, 2018, https://asunow.asu.edu/20180411-discoveries-asu-research-shelter-dog-welfare-lisa-gunter.

11   Greguska, "Giving pound puppies a paw up."

CHAPTER TWELVE
BREED DISCRIMINATION

Audiences of all ages have enjoyed watching *Lady and the Tramp*, the cute animated movie of two dogs in love, despite their breed differences. Yet another production, *The Doberman Gang*, first released in 1972, depicts Dobermans robbing a bank and includes imagery of rather fierce faces on what in real life are charming and placid dogs.

Let's not be misled by the theatrics of movies and film to prejudice against certain breeds. It's a different story if you've personally experienced a real-life episode with an aggressive dog. I'm guessing if that is the case, the dog was probably off leash and not under the owner's control.

I'm surprised by the number of folks who are afraid of Dobermans, and I often wonder if those early movies didn't create an unfair bias.

One of my regular clients is Assisi, a four-year-old Doberman, and a saint. His staycations have never been anything but delightful and normal. He loves to play with other dogs of all sizes and ages, shows considerable restraint around children, and especially enjoys cuddling on the couch. He has the personality of a Golden Retriever and will relentlessly beg for loving pets and hugs all day, and he never tires of them when provided.

Because we sleep under ceiling fans, necessary in the Arizona climate, my son and I bundle Assisi under the covers to keep his ears from getting cold. We treat him like a baby, and his sweet nature shows it. His mom and I are good friends, so I can confidently report that Linda and Assisi are regulars at a local dog park and Assisi has never instigated unruly behavior nor attempted robbery of positive pack play. To know him is to love him.

Assisi – the Saintly Doberman

The Doberman Pinscher originated in Germany in the late 1800s and is named for Louis Dobermann, a tax collector who desired a guard dog to accompany him while making his rounds. He crossed a German Shepherd with a German Pinscher; DNA of Manchester Terrier, Weimaraner, and Greyhound were later added to the mix. Today's version is an alert guard dog and family protector who also demonstrates an adventurous spirit and eager-to-please disposition.

I have only had the pleasure of hosting one other Doberman, Belle, who is the biggest scaredy-cat I know. Belle is extremely shy and takes a bit of coaxing to warm up to new people. When we first met, her acute timidity prompted me to reduce all noise in my home, sometimes banishing it altogether. I purposely held off running appliances including the dishwasher, blender, washer, dryer, and noisy ice maker and added soft Mozart in the background.

In the beginning, she planted herself firmly on a rug in the kitchen and rarely strayed beyond her declared space. I tiptoed around her until she felt safe and comfortable in my presence and finally followed me from room to room. This quiet accommodation continued for months. Her favorite spot was under my office desk.

When my home was under contract for sale, Belle was in residence the day the bank's appraiser arrived to take photos. She would not come out from under the desk, despite our now-established friendship and my coaxing and pleading with treats. The appraiser grew impatient with her unwillingness to relocate her position, so he thrust his camera at me to take the final photo needed for his report. I can only imagine the bank underwriter's surprised smile while reviewing the picture of a scared Doberman staring back.

Public perception of presumed aggressive breeds is not limited to Dobermans. The German Shepherd, Rottweiler, Jack Russell Terrier, American Bulldog, Bull Terrier, Chow, and Bull Mastiff, among others, are equally discriminated against.

The Pit Bull and Staffordshire Terrier are at the top of this discriminatory dog chain. Over 900 cities have laws banning or restricting "aggressive" breeds, such as mandatory sterilization of Pit Bulls in many counties throughout California. In addition, most homeowner's insurance companies exclude coverage for these breed types.

Sadly, this wonderful breed has been exploited by greedy dog fighters—to the chagrin of those who have learned that with proper and early socialization, devotion, and love, this is a wonderful and protective family companion.

Any dog is capable of negative behavior under a myriad of circumstances, and those who have been mistreated by their owners are more prone to evasive maneuvers in the interest of preservation and self-defense. Children need supervision and instruction regarding proper care and interaction to avoid sparking a dog's defensive reactions if poked or prodded in the wrong way.

Dogs that are ill often react with added crankiness. Are you happy when you're sick?

Unintentional or poor breeding can also affect the DNA of any dog who suddenly goes rogue.

Use your best judgment when choosing the right breed for your family, while also withholding judgment against breeds you haven't met or owned.

CHAPTER THIRTEEN
GAME OF CONES

Jeri and Mike's preparation as future dog hosts began years before I met them. They are particularly adept with exuberant breeds, including the Siberian Husky, a very active dog. Think about this: Huskies are bred to sled across miles of Arctic tundra and will race for days with unending enthusiasm and endurance. This breed needs significant daily exercise and is not recommended for inactive owners.

As Jeri tells it, their beloved Husky, Blizzard, blew his knee at the age of three and required ACL surgery. Although it's a common malady and requires a relatively simple surgical procedure, they encountered an unusual post-op reaction. "When Mike and I arrived to fetch Blizzard from the vet, we were met by nervous staff, one of whom actually whispered in confession: 'We are having trouble getting him ready.'"

Mike and Jeri heard for themselves as they neared the recovery room where Blizzard was howling his heart out. Two technicians were standing outside his cage in deep discussion; the veterinarian seemed equally perplexed. He suggested a sling to help carry Blizzard to the car, while strong pain medications were thrust into their hands (at no charge).

Michael, a now-retired police sergeant with professional experience dealing with extreme rescues requiring split-second decisions, simply scooped Blizzard into his arms. The ensuing silence was golden.

Blizzard was cool as long as he was touched … all day, every day, for the next four days. Jeri spent the recuperation period sleeping on the dog bed with a hand or arm around Blizzard as often as possible. "If I fell asleep and my hand slipped, he howled. If I went to the bathroom, more howling. Get up to grab a sandwich. Howling. As long as he felt my hand on him, he was quiet and content."

While many dogs may require surgery, with or without a "halo" to accompany forced rest and medications, Blizzard demonstrated the best recuperative measure of all: human comfort and touch.

Jeri and Mike continue to work energetically to entertain dogs in their home, especially with the agile breeds. With two acres of secure backyard, their home is a dog's Promised Land, complete with a swimming pool, agility equipment, and a boat. They are my go-to nannies for energetic, adventurous, and athletic dogs.

This does not exclude their small-dog guests or the owner-described "chair warmers" that suddenly run wild when given vast outdoor room to roam freely and explore new smells and activities outside of their own home.

Luna, a three-year-old former racing Greyhound, is a frequent flier in their home. They initially expected she would lounge around, now comfortable in her retirement—provided she didn't encounter a wild bunny that might trigger a flashback.

Her first visit defied all laws of gravity. Jeri created an obstacle course for Luna in their backyard playground, and Luna's spirited personality emerged, revealing a dog that was still determined to win the race. She needed little coaching to vault through the hoops, high jump over poles, and perform her own tour jete, leaping and turning in every direction. While we routinely text our pet parents with updates on their dog's staycation activities, Jeri likes to create videos of her guests, including props for added visual entertainment.

I've had the pleasure of entertaining Luna, and given my small graveled backyard, I could only offer her long outdoor walks for exercise. Despite her high-speed sprinting skills, our outdoor strolls together were as calm as the Dead Sea. She qualifies for the high-heel-worthy club. I could have been in three-inch stilettos as she patiently padded by my side.

The Greyhound, classified as a sight hound, began its ascension in Britain during the Anglo-Saxon period, favored by both commoners and nobility as a breed who could run after and out-chase game. Coursing for hare became a common sport, with the Greyhound providing entertainment for the upper class. When emigrated to the US, the Greyhound's distance-running abilities landed the breed on tracks chasing mechanical rabbits. Thus, track racing was born, sadly relegating the Greyhound to profit-making "property."

They are affectionately referred to as "the world's fastest couch potato." They have a calm, gentle nature and love to lounge quietly indoors, but they'll gallop when given outdoor space. Luna clearly demonstrated this unique breed characteristic given the disparate boarding landscapes offered by Jeri and me.

Luna the Greyhound and her owners

Luna and her Superhero Nannies

CHAPTER FOURTEEN

DAILY EXERCISE AND MENTAL STIMULATION—KEYS TO HAPPINESS

Just as human children need the stimulation of extracurricular activities like summer camps and after-school activities, all dogs need mental stimulation and exercise to eliminate boredom.

Original breeds were developed with some job in mind: to herd, to hunt, to retrieve, to rescue, to guard, or to protect. As most dogs now reside in urban developments and are kept indoors, pent-up energy can lead to unwanted behavioral problems.

It's important to provide regular activities that promote happy canine campers. Take your dog to a dog park, enroll him in doggie day care or specialty classes, or play games with her at home to help enhance your dog's daily life.

While most dogs can get by with thirty minutes of daily exercise, super-active sporting and hunting breeds require more strenuous activity for longer stretches. Running, jogging, and hiking should be incorporated into your daily agenda with these furry athletes.

Because your dog's exercise regimen is often hindered by inclement weather, activity boxes are springing up on the retail market designed to entertain your dog year-round and especially in hot summer or cold winter months when you're trapped indoors. These ship-to-your-door gift box ensembles are packed with treats and toys from the creative thinkers at PupBox, Bullymake, KONG and others. Some are customized for the unique needs of various dog breeds and sizes. No assembly required, and only minimal parent participation past the click of your online order and spectating supervision.

Check out these fun companies for festive in-home entertainment, and apply the coupon code offers below with your purchase:

FOR KONG: Use "DOOLITTLE5" to get $5 off your purchase at https://kongbox.com/discount/DOOLITTLE5.

There's no expiration date. One coupon per use per customer.

FOR BULLYMAKE: Use "DOOLITTLE10" to get $10 off your purchase at bullymake.com.

Enter your promo code at the top of the checkout page.

FOR PUPBOX: Pupscribers use "ACCORDINGTODOG" to get $20 off your first PupBox on any subscription plan at https://pupbox.com/.

There is no expiration date. One coupon per use per customer.

You can also design your own indoor games and activities using common household items. These unbelievably simple ideas are equally effective and easy on the budget:

1. A muffin tin and balls:

Hide treats at the bottom of each "cupcake" hole. Place plastic balls or tennis balls on top and present on the floor. Your dog has to use her nose to nuzzle the ball away in order to find the hidden prize. Inexpensive muffin tins and tennis balls can be found at Dollar Tree or 99 Cent Stores. You may need to alternate the type of treats or balls to keep the novelty alive.

2. Empty water bottle and a sock:

Fit a tube sock over a squeaky water bottle, tie a knot at the top, and let Fido go at it! Most dogs love the sound of squeaky toys, and many will do their best to destroy the toy until the noise-making object is found. The entire bottle IS the noise-making object, so it should provide lasting entertainment, unless you own a dog with jaws of steel. If this is the case, do NOT try this at home. Note to those owners in this category: *Bullymake* boxes cater to voracious chewers.

3. Baby-bottle treat dispenser:

Cut the top of the nipple from a plastic baby bottle and add small enough treats in the bottom of the bottle to allow their escape. As your dog chases the bottle around the room, the goodies spill out in the process.

4. The indubitable value of a KONG:

This is a must-have for every dog owner. They're available in all sizes, shaped like a triple-scoop ice-cream cone, and most enjoyed when stuffed with treats or peanut butter (better yet: freeze the peanut butter for a longer-lasting experience). The KONG provides fun entertainment and is also a useful training tool for dogs who like to chew on things, especially puppies. Instead of letting your pup munch on your shoes, make a trade with a KONG instead. For added mental enrichment, hide a treat-filled KONG or two around the house to create a treasure hunt for your dog.

5. Hula hoops and poles:

This is a simple way to test your dog's inner agility. Start with either a hula hoop or broomstick if you have a helper to hold the other end. Keep them low to the ground at first and encourage your dog to run through the hoop or jump over the pole. Reward each successful maneuver with a treat. Continue this game and increase the challenge by elevating the height just slightly.

6. Large bucket and a ball:

Play basketball with your wannabe jock! Using a wide pail or bucket, drop a small ball inside with the command "dunk." Lead your dog to the bucket, point, and repeat "dunk." When your dog catches on and drops the ball in the "basket," immediately offer a treat with praise. Second quarter of this basketball game includes tossing the ball farther away from the basket so your dog has to run down the court to make the score. Continue to offer treats and/or praise each time his attempts are successful.

I love the dogs that soft mouth a plush toy or carry it around to show off or present it as a "gift" to you. To a Golden Retriever or Labrador, this special presentation might represent the hunter's felled target she was bred to retrieve for you. Other dogs are determined to attack and shred, particularly if there is a squeaky item that must be eliminated. I've seen dogs with strength to rival "Jaws of Life" shred and dismantle a massive ball of dense plastic. Dogs can accidentally consume plastic parts or stuffing, so always supervise your dog around toys.

These simple ideas, in combination with your supervision and engagement, are very small investments to keep a dog's mind, body, and spirit active and to extinguish ennui.

CHAPTER FIFTEEN

ALOHA! APPLYING FOR A POOCH PASSPORT TO HAWAII

I'm always up for a challenge, which presented in an entertaining petition from Chris and her two dogs, who required boarding for two months while she relocated to Hawaii. Given the very strict protocols on the island, Chris had started their quarantine process yet was running out of time and needed our help.

One of my nannies, Jamie, and I embraced this assignment, which extended beyond just sixty days of boarding. Chris left for Hawaii, and we were tasked with completing final checklist items.

This included a trip to the vet for a wellness exam with proper health certificates, written in strict verbiage with specific brand-name vaccinations. We also assumed the role of booking agent with Hawaiian Airlines. There were only three spaces available in Hawaiian Airlines' cargo hold, and we needed two of them. Jamie and I synchronized our call for their flight reservation, which had to occur on a specific date (*exactly* thirty days prior to departure) and be coordinated with precision due to the difference in time zones.

Following all of that, Jamie and her family drove our furry charges to San Diego from Phoenix, a six-hour drive, as the warm weather in Arizona prohibited a direct flight to Hawaii in May.

I'd had my share of complicated mortgage loans in the past, so this scenario was not that difficult for me, and I was boosted tremendously by a very organized and committed dog mom, along with Jamie's willingness to comply with it all. The dogs were successfully reunited with Chris in time for Mother's Day.

While flying with your dogs is not that difficult, Chris had to fly solo. The Hawaii Department of Agriculture zealously guards its "rabies-free" island status with understandably strict protocols.

During our vet visit, it was mentioned that one dog owner, wishing to circumvent these strict protocols, attempted to sneak their dog on a flight bound for Hawaii. The dog's presence was discovered mid-flight, which required a mandatory return to the original airport. I can't imagine the distress of the other passengers at this idiotic delay of their travel plans.

If you intend to fly with your dog, your option of cabin or cargo hold will be based largely on the size, age, and breed of your dog. Generally, dogs over 20 pounds are too big to fit under the seat, so they must go in cargo, provided the airline has a pressurized system to support it. An exception is made, of course, for therapy animals.

Recent turbulence between airlines and animal-toting passengers has caused the commercial airline industry to reevaluate guidelines. Many are caught in a tailspin regarding what constitutes a therapy or emotional support animal and how to identify those that provide psychological service versus imposters paraded by their owners for the purpose of obtaining free carry-on passage.

Trained service animals are a different class of airline traveler and are accepted in cabin space for owners with disabilities. These special service dogs provide critical life-functioning assistance for those with visual, hearing, or mobility limitations and are trained to be non-reactive.

As the Department of Transportation grapples with this delicate debate, it's best to ditch the fake "Service Animal" vest, which is used at the expense of those who truly deserve to fly free, like Daniel the emotional support duck.

No one cried foul when this unique passenger, outfitted in red shoes and a Captain America diaper, made his aviation debut two years ago with his owner, Carla Fitzgerald, who suffers from PTSD. Carla proved her conscientiousness by strapping on a specially designed diaper harness and bathing Daniel before the flight.

This unflappable duck, adopted at two days old, has helped Carla recover from a harrowing accident that left her immobilized for several months; she continues to live with pain and PTSD today. It should also be noted that Daniel is an Indian Runner duck, a breed that does not fly … unless traveling on a commercial plane.

For helpful tips regarding flight protocols and a list of professional pet-travel companies, visit https://www.ipata.org. IPATA is a non-profit trade association of independent members dedicated to the safe and humane transportation of pets and animals. This includes ground and air transportation specialists who can assist you with your precious cargo within the US and abroad.

CHAPTER SIXTEEN
CREATING MARY PUPPINS

As our company's reputation for spoiling pets grew, it became clear that families with multiple dogs, cats, birds, fish, or animals with special needs would fare better with a move-in nanny. I flew with the idea, and after adding some document legalese and bonding insurance, I rounded up folks who could pack their bags and travel to clients' homes. *Mary Puppins has arrived!*

Our first move-in request came during the summer of 2014 from a family with four dogs and two cats needing a weeklong stay. I immediately called Charlene, who wrote in her bio: "Have you heard the song by the Pointer Sisters, 'I'm So Excited'?" Her enthusiasm for every pet job has never wavered.

We successfully catered to this dynamic household of mixed breeds and soon went on to acquire more clients with a houseful of fur and sometimes feathers. The next family, with a Conure Parrot, was an adventure and required a nanny with nun-like patience. Charlene filled the bill, and when I would call to check on her welfare, the background noise was akin to what you'd hear in a pet store aviary.

While I thoroughly enjoy listening to wild birds singing, words cannot describe the cry of a large caged bird inside the house. Conures live twenty to forty years and do not sing per se—this is a bird with a megaphone.

While every owner of a Pekingese, Pug, Bulldog, Boston Terrier, Boxer, Shih Tzu, or any deep-in-their-sleep snoring dog would not flinch at the sound of their canine lumberjacks cutting logs, these specific birds are unusual; their sounds require some getting used to.

No offense meant to any bird-owning parent who lovingly dotes on their feathery friend. As a pet-care provider, it takes resilience and a good pair of earplugs to share that love.

Most of our move-in clients are dogs who don't navigate unfamiliar surroundings well, multiple pets who can't be easily packed up and brought to our homes, or homeowners who want their house kept safe and tidy too.

We've had requests to walk our charges up to four times a day; drive them twice daily to a local park so they could potty on familiar gravel; sleep on a floor mattress (for the senior dog who couldn't climb stairs and lived in a house that lacked a bedroom on the first floor); administer a myriad of medications that required an all-day diary of "pooch pill" protocols; pick up fallen fruit in the backyard so it wasn't consumed as canine dessert (this includes swift removal of the fruit of a dog for those suffering with coprophagia[12]); get up at 4:00 a.m. (for check-in, as the parents left for their ridiculously early flights OR to let the senior dogs out to pee at that hour); rinse off and towel dry the swimmers and thwart those that aspire to become swimmers; create unique barricades for the devious diggers and escape artists; guard the home and engineer the smart ones (some homes and appliances are smarter than mere mortals); and greet contractors, landscapers, and pool peeps with flair that would rival Mrs. Doubtfire.

Nancy, a Doolittle's Doghouse nanny who boards in her home, has a regular houseguest named Pixie, a "pistol-packing" Whoodle[13] puppy who is very vocal when she's ramping up with Nancy's pup, Pearson. Nancy works from home and frequently moderates and participates in teleconferences and webinars that require clear audio without background noise. Rather than cancel Pixie's playdates during these

---

12 Coprophagia: eating feces or dung.

13 Whoodle: a dog bred from the Wheaten Terrier and Poodle.

scheduled performances that require a quiet workspace, she creates a "remote" office to quell the noise.

On one occasion, armed with her travel coffee mug, Nancy drove to the Dillard's Fashion Square Mall parking garage. It was before store hours, so she thought it would be nice and quiet. Upon arrival, having added extra time for her reconnaissance, she discovered major construction disturbance, which required a detour to an adjacent parking lot with less traffic noise. After considerable shifting of gears, she repositioned her car seat to accommodate her laptop and presentation materials and settled in. Her webinar "audience" never knew she was sitting in her car at a shopping mall!

This is five-star pet sitter performance at its finest. You name it we've done it in the interest of providing pampered pet care.

The reality is, we're doing everything it takes to love and care for your pets because that's what YOU do! We cater to thousands of clients, and close to 75% of them allow their dogs in their bed. I don't have a problem with that, and neither do most of my nannies. We're past Victoria Secret lingerie, and a live pillow to snuggle with is a bonus for us; it's helpful if our snoozing partners have been recently groomed and practice good dental hygiene at home.

During first-time client calls, we ask a myriad of questions to determine how to meet expectations based on pooch proclivities and protocols. These daily conversations often resemble confessions, in which clients divulge their secrets with a twinge of guilt and the unspoken question: "Do you think I'm crazy because I love my dog more than (*fill in the blank)*?"

Please do not think you're alone if you are head over tail in love with your dog. I thought I was the only one hopelessly in love with dogs until I began boarding them and gathered other huge crazy-for-dog fans to the arena. If you aren't spoiling your pets and treating them with equality in your home, you wouldn't be calling us, nor would you be fully enjoying life with your dog.

Pop quiz:

Q: What do you do when you find a dog sleeping on your bed?

A: Move to the other side or go to the sofa!

Many of us find ourselves sleeping in contorted positions on our beds to accommodate the sprawling foot warmers.

Despite some experts' claims that you should never let your dog sleep in your bed—as you should be the dominant member of the pack—it's your dog, your life, your bedsheets, and your choice. At a minimum, providing a bed for them on your bedroom floor is always a great way to bond with your dog and has the added bonus of nighttime security at your feet.

If your dog uses her front paws to vigorously rearrange the covers, fluff her pet blanket, or similarly dig away at the couch, she is creating a "softer" spot to lie down, much like her wolf ancestors did in the wild. It was necessary for them to shovel away the bramble to more comfortably tuck in after a day of hunting and surviving. If not using their front paws as a pickaxe, they might simply circle three times before lying down, another ancestral ritual that survives today.

CHAPTER SEVENTEEN
DON'T LEAVE ME OUT IN THE COLD!

As a responsible pet parent, you are making a lifetime commitment to your dog. At least I hope you are. Dogs are born with a natural ability to figure things out fast, and they have an inherent desire to please if treated with equal opportunity in your home.

Before I began boarding dogs, an early experience with an inexperienced pet parent occurred by happenstance in my neighborhood. A small older dog, known as Benji yet nicknamed "Jesus" by his mom, was left in the backyard often—for days at a time and with potato chips and Oreo cookies for food. This was not an equal relationship and bears witness to the reality that some people shouldn't own pets.

I had heard odd stories from the next-door neighbor about this pet mom's peculiar behavior and oblivion, yet it wasn't until I walked by her house one day—it was Valentine's Day by coincidence—that I truly understood. Jesus was barking woefully outside. His bark was just different. It spoke to me in a way I can't describe. I was drawn to the unlocked backyard gate, and without hesitation, I helped myself, scooped him up, and brought him to my home. I put a note on the door: "I have your dog. Call me." I also left my address and phone number.

Jesus was given love and proper food in my home and, after marking the living room couch *only once,* he settled in quickly and happily. This little valentine was content to be inside a home with curious and cordial canines for additional comfort.

After several days went by without a call from the owner, I contacted Phoenix Animal Care and Control to confirm that the dog was considered abandoned and I had the freedom to claim ownership. I took him to my favorite groomer; he was a mess from living outside.

Judy Wolfe is a magician with scissors, in addition to being a fierce animal advocate and dog whisperer. Jesus was transformed from a mangy, dirty pile of matted fur into a white, beautiful lamb. When I explained the circumstances to Judy, she offered her services for free. I left her salon in tears of joy.

Now convinced I was doing the right thing, my next stop was the vet. Dr. Soltero Sr. performed a complete well exam and, with the exception of pointing out serious dental issues, proclaimed him to be in good health. While I was prepared to pay him for his services, with only casual mention of his story, Dr. Soltero also waived his bill (more tears).

As I was fully committed to the care and control of Jesus, I began the search for a permanent home. At the time, I had two dogs of my own and a three-year-old son to nurture. I considered my list of friends who might want a companion animal.

Don lived next door and catered to senior citizens as a professional financial planner. Blessedly, he had a client who had recently lost her dog, so he arranged a blind date for the two of them.

I only had a few weeks with this marvelous dog in my home, and as he skipped happily away with Don on the day of departure, I knew that I had done the right thing and that Jesus was about to find heaven.

I spoke to the new owner shortly after this matchmaking experience. Despite her fixed income, she paid $600 to have his bad teeth removed; they were sleeping closely together, and she couldn't stand his breath! Jesus no longer slept outside alone, and this delightful widow found her perfect companion.

CHAPTER EIGHTEEN
TAKE ME AS I AM

A few takeaways from my theft of Benji include the fact that he only marked my home once. As Judy explained to me, he simply wanted to say, "Let me have this one spot to call my own because I need a real home."

Don't be discouraged by dogs that mark indoors. Intentional marking is separate from indiscriminate accidents (an especially frequent occurrence with houseguests who are pee pad trained, puppies in training, incontinent seniors, or super submissive or overly excited dogs who release on sight).

Male dogs are more apt to mark indoors, particularly if they are still intact. Promoted by the smell of another dog's scent, this inclination to lift and spray is akin to leaving their business card in a male-dominant gesture of exchange. Despite the wonderful odor-eliminating products on the market, once a chair or sofa has been marked, it will scream "I'm a fire hydrant." Following strenuous or professional cleaning, try covering the furniture with a bedsheet to create a scent barrier. Lining the bottom of your furniture with aluminum foil might help. While unsightly to you, the startling sound of his "water" against the foil might stop this behavior.

Neutering your male dogs early is the best offense to indoor marking.

Often, adding another pet or new roommate to the household can promote marking. Your dog may be establishing his territory. This scenario may require that you honor his delegated space or favorite couch, chair, or targeted object while ushering the others to a separate area until they find peace together.

If chronic marking persists, contact a local dog trainer for assistance, or resign to diapering your dog while he is inside. He may outgrow it or realize that the diapers aren't fun after all. If not, please invest in disposable pet diapers and accept what is.

Pee pad training is discouraged, as it's difficult for a dog to differentiate between a cotton pee pad and a household rug. Dogs should be given the opportunity to whizz outside to spread their business cards around the neighborhood. The transference of pee pad locations from your home to ours is often confusing and typically results in our houseguests "missing their mark." While lifestyle circumstances might require pee pads for your dog's toilet, if you work crazy-long hours and this is the only relief method for your dog, let's rethink what's in the pet's best interest.

Regardless of owner circumstances, no dog should be surrendered because they are "acting up" nor should any dog be kept outside and deprived of human companionship. Ever.

CHAPTER NINETEEN
COMBATTING CRUELTY TO ANIMALS

To those of us who are not actively engaged in animal rescue, if you witness abuse, abandonment, neglect of any animal—domesticated or not—PLEASE DO SOMETHING ABOUT IT. There are far too many abandoned and abused pets. The statistics are staggering.

According to forallanimals.org:

> Psychologists and social workers understand that animal cruelty, domestic violence, elder abuse, and child abuse intersect. Taking animal cruelty seriously actually puts law enforcement and prosecutors in a better position to uncover other crimes. Animal abuse is a significant indicator that there is something wrong in the abuser's home or life. Sometimes animal cruelty is more visible to neighbors (such as leaving a dog tethered in the cold) than human violence. An animal control officer might be the only person who can uncover other crimes and alert authorities.[14]

We have a moral responsibility to protect not only our urban environments but also those creatures that can't protect themselves. I quote Arthur Schopenhauer, who best describes my uncompromising position about animal cruelty: "Compassion for animals is intimately connected with goodness of character, and it may be confidently asserted that he who is cruel to living creatures cannot be a good man."[15]

---

14   "Animal Cruelty, Law Enforcement, and Prosecution – Faqs," For All Animals, accessed December 3, 2018, https://www.forallanimals.org/animal-cruelty-law-enforcement-and-prosecution-faqs/.

15   Arthur Schopenhauer, *The Basis of Morality* (Macmillan Company, 1915), 223.

If you feel the same way, please join me and other animal advocates by taking action on behalf of those animals subjected to cruelty by those who lack good moral character.

You can subscribe to and support the Animal Legal Defense Fund at https://aldf.org. Follow their newsletters and social media announcements regarding pending court cases and legal action against all perpetrators of animal abuse.

Donate to their efforts, which run the gamut of animal rights support, ranging from the fight against inhumane agricultural and commercial interests—including road-show rodeos and irresponsible zookeepers—to overly zealous trophy hunters and puppy mill operators.

As a society, we need to collectively advocate for harsher sentences for people found guilty of domestic animal abuse. Their motto is simple: Abuse an Animal—Go to Jail. There should be no get-out-of-jail-free card in this regard.

Some recent examples of their extraordinary work include collaboration with California State Senator Scott Wilk, R-Santa Clarita, jointly proposing the "Animal Welfare and Violence Intervention Act of 2018." This valuable legislation, known as Senate Bill 1024, was unanimously passed by the Assembly Committee on Public Safety to *require mental health evaluation and education, if not counseling, for convicted animal abusers.*

The ALDF has successfully negotiated settlements with certain pet stores selling sick dogs and some puppy mill operators posing as "professional breeders." The only way to shut down this industry is to target the contemptible mill operators and irresponsible retailers.

Several cases have been filed by the ALDF against roadside zoo operators who are violating the Endangered Species Act and anti-cruelty laws. An ongoing campaign with significant implications for our future as a moral society is #NotProperty: we must recognize that all animals, domesticated or not, should be treated as living beings and not property.

These legal beagles need our support.

You may also consider joining forces with the Humane Society of the United States and ASPCA, including their local chapters in desperate need of volunteers and fosters.

Entertain the idea of volunteering to help a local shelter with their pets or administrative needs, and enlist your friends and family to join you in this worthwhile endeavor.

You might be a good candidate to serve as a foster parent, temporarily housing a dog or cat. A well-organized shelter will equip you with tools and tips as to what to expect. This is a great way to introduce a pet into your home or to your children if you haven't embraced the permanent commitment to a companion animal and need to dip your toe in the water before you take the plunge as a full-time pet parent.

If you are grieving the loss of a pet, what better way to soothe your soul than to assist a shelter pet who needs you as much as you need them for solace?

The Humane Society of the United States is equally diligent in the quest to uncover abusive puppy mill operators. These shameful commercial breeders typically subject their breeding dogs and litters to unfathomable and inhumane conditions. Support the Humane Society's efforts with donations, and *please don't buy a puppy from a pet store.* While more communities are passing laws prohibiting pet stores from selling dogs from puppy mills, it remains a long road toward progress. Yet, it's one worth traveling together.

DoSomething.org, "a global movement for good," boasts an impressive online movement with over 5 million followers. Visit their website for an engaging snapshot of youthful exuberance, spearheaded by Millennials making pawsitive differences. While these passionate organizers have many campaign messages and ideas, there is a special section for animals, and an invitation to launch your own campaign.

Mercyforanimals.org is another excellent resource. I hope you'll follow, support, and/or join this impressive coalition of animal activists and investigators committed to protecting farm animals.

Follow Change.org and their specific animal-related petitions. This is an impressive platform for positive change across the globe. Over 250,000 people rallied around a ballot petition to raise awareness of the abusive practices meted upon racing Greyhounds, specifically in Florida. Florida citizens recently cast their public vote in support of Amendment 13. This initiative, sponsored and supported by GREY2K USA Worldwide, the Humane Society of the United States, the Doris Day Animal League and Animal Wellness Action, was immensely successful with 69% of the public vote approving the measure. This historic movement now mandates by law that every dog racetrack in Florida (there are eleven) must ring their last bell by January 2021.

Statistically speaking, dogs are the most abused animal, representing 64% of reported cruelty cases according to dopplr.com, a legal research group.[16] And they can't speak for themselves. Animal abuse is a crime in every state, yet most state laws are outdated, punishing offenders with a mere slap on the wrist.

Until that changes, if you witness animal cruelty, at least pick up the phone. Anyone can call their local animal control authorities,

---

16   B. Clausen, "Animal Cruelty Laws by State: Is It a Crime to Abuse an Animal," Dopplr, March 29, 2016, https://www.dopplr.com/animal-cruely-laws/.

law enforcement, or 911. You can also report suspected cases of abuse to your local Humane Society chapter or ALDF by calling 707-795-2533.

As Gandhi so eloquently stated, "Be the change you wish to see in the world." Positive change occurs when passionate people raise their voice and unite in causes that are honorable and just.

CHAPTER TWENTY
ROUTINES ARE IMPORTANT TO A DOG

Life happens, and sudden changes are often unavoidable. It's easy for us to nurture a dog through a short-term change in their routine when they arrive for a boarding experience. Following a pre-scheduled introduction, our prospective guest has had a chance to sniff us out first before moving into our home for a fixed period of time ranging from several days to several weeks. After their first staycation experience, our repeat guests run to our doors with happy tails and excitement. And they always know Mom or Dad is going to pick them up. This becomes their new norm when their owners are traveling.

Extreme and more permanent adjustments in routines, however, are hugely upsetting to dogs. This includes a house move, loss of a guardian or fellow furry companion, and seasonal changes. This often happens in families with school-age children. Back-to-school blues not only affect your human kids but your dog too. The end of summer break is stressful for pets as their human companions adjust their routines.

Pet parents should be acutely aware of the depressing effect such changes have on dogs that are used to constant attention and activity and now face an emptier household because the kids are in school, their companions are gone, or the household dynamics have materially changed.

Most dogs will show demonstrable signs of melancholy when a companion animal passes. They may keep looking for them in rooms or the outdoor places you visited while on a walk. You may notice a change in their vocalization, from sudden and frequent whining to louder or more muted speech. They may eat less, sleep more, demand greater attention from you, and/or appear more anxious.

If they are now the only dog in the home, it may seem to you that they aren't reacting at all, perhaps because they've assumed a new role that includes consoling you while simultaneously assuming the alpha position. Or maybe they really love being the only child.

During these events of inconstancy, it's important to pay close attention to your dog's feelings—he loves his comfortable spaces and faithful companions and will miss them when they're gone.

Any "new" behaviors are your cues to *focus on Fido* and help him adjust to life's detours. To get a jump-start on building new roads together, consider the following suggestions:

1. Enroll your dog in doggie day care or hire a pet sitter or dog walker to break up the day with fun activity, exercise, and mental enrichment.

2. Purchase the Petcube Camera, or similar nanny cam, as an option to keep an eye on your dog when you're not at home. The Petcube Camera has interactive capability and allows you to observe and talk to your dog when you're not home. A laser option is included, a feature you can activate remotely to give your dog or cat a chase around the room. The Petcube Bites Treat Camera is especially fun—it has a unique food-dispensing function that allows you to remotely launch treats for your pet's tasty entertainment as he chases down the kibble missiles.

3. Leave an old T-shirt lying around for your dog to sniff and "sense" his loved ones in their absence. Dogs love your smell so much it might explain why they fondle your socks and underwear.

4. Always, always, always strive to provide daily exercise for your dog.

5. Provide an outdoor view from an indoor window so your dog can observe neighborhood activity. Obviously, if she is barking excessively and annoying your neighbors, or if she's the type to lunge at the mailman or UPS driver, you'll have to shutter the shutters. I have personally found that most dogs enjoy peering through my windows. It's reminiscent of Mrs. Kravitz[17] yet can be mildly entertaining for them to spy on people, bunnies, and birds. I personally benefit by their bark alerts, as I live alone and am not prone to answering the door if company is not expected. The sight of a barking dog through an open window is a great deterrent for unwanted solicitors or would-be robbers.

6. Bring your dog with you as much as possible. Short field trips to dog-friendly patios and stores, farmers markets, outdoor events, and drive-through errands are just a few examples of easy ways to include your dog.

7. Turn on the TV or radio when you leave. Classical music is the best option, as most dogs don't love rock 'n' roll or shows that involve loud and frightening noises. A popular television channel built specifically for the canine audience is DOG TV. Based on extensive scientific research, DOG TV offers three content segments to choose from: RELAXATION, STIM-ULATION, & EXPOSURE. These programs are tailored to your individual dog's needs and aim to eliminate boredom, anxiety, and depression. For a free 30-day trial of DOG TV, please tune in via this link: http://dogtv.refr.cc/tori01.

---

17 Gladys Kravitz was a fictional character played by Alice Pearce in the 1964 TV series Bewitched. She was cast as the nosy neighbor.

Stay the course and be as present, affectionate, and reassuring as possible during those life-changing chapters that affect all members of the family.

CHAPTER TWENTY-ONE
RESCUE ME SO I CAN BE THE BEST I'M MEANT TO BE

All dogs are born with a strong desire to partner with us; their devotion is unmatched in human alliances. A dog will never complain that they had a bad day at the office or at school. They will whine and whimper for various reasons, yet I've never seen a dog throw a temper tantrum. Most of them will tolerate our giddy ideas to dress them up at Halloween and not worry if their outfit makes their butt look big. They simply go along in order to belong.

Given the privilege to host other people's dogs, I have met just about every breed—purebred and not-so-sure bred. I have never met a dog I didn't like.

While I can make some assumptions about individual breed characteristics and prepare for what might typically follow (genetically speaking), some of the best surprises have been the rescued dogs. More than once, I've found they have a more pronounced attitude of gratitude.

Cole was found foraging on the streets of LA and brought into an office by a Good Samaritan. He had no identification or chip, which launched a company collaboration to find a solution.

A coworker was present during Cole's debut and immediately called his wife, with a childlike plea: "Can we keep him?" Cole was approximately six months old then and quickly wiggled into Mike's heart.

Cole is a treasure of a dog with exquisite manners. He has that innate sixth sense all dogs possess, knowing when to be gentle and bow in the presence of children. He will play and run with other dogs if invited and also understands if another pooch doesn't want to party and needs to be left alone. Obedient and patient, loving and smart, Cole is a happy dog who makes others happy in his presence.

His eating habits are slightly unusual, as his new parents quickly discovered. Following months of dogged determination, they cracked the code. As Cole wasn't particularly interested in food, given an unknown period of time scrounging for a meal, his new mom finally found a recipe that worked... and inadvertently discovered that a paper plate was his preferred serving dish.

While entertaining Cole in my home, with a stack of paper plates and cooked hamburger and rice, it became obvious to me that Cole also needed a quiet kitchen without distraction during mealtime.

The slightest sound or movement would derail him from eating. This didn't mean he was full; he was simply investigating the source of the noise. When satisfied, deeming the "all clear," Cole would return to his food. I would patiently wait for him to complete his reconnaissance. I'd take a seat on the floor and sometimes coax him back with a food offering from my hand.

I am convinced this dietary procession is a result of his former street life. Imagine the noise associated with the bang and clang of dumpsters and cars whizzing by on the LA freeway; I can't help conjuring the cartoon image of a restaurateur throwing a shoe at him.

Perhaps his best meals were found on paper plates in public garbage bins or inside discarded McDonald's wrappers. Maybe a warm-hearted restaurant cook put leftovers in a to-go bag outside. It doesn't matter. Paper plates are easy to come by. And I no longer have to sit on the floor and wait.

Cole has taught all of us not only the importance of patience and perseverance, but also how to dig deeper into the mind of a dog and his memories. Because of his caregivers' committed fortitude to nurture his unique cuisine preferences, Cole has brought considerable happiness to his family's table. Mike and his wife, Dana, can't imagine life without him.

Cole and his paper plate

A good friend and neighbor, Janet, is a fierce proponent of adoption. In the eighteen years I've known her, all but one of her furry companions have been rescues. Her current lovebug, Mandy, came from a hoarder's home. Given there were twenty-four Shih Tzus running amok, I'm fairly certain there was considerable inbreeding going on. Mandy was born with irregular joint development and unusually truncated front legs that resemble flippers. This little "dolphin" is the sweetest dog ever and just loves to snuggle.

Her gait is analogous to a drunken sailor trying to find purchase. Yet, the smell of her food will prompt her to sprint without a hitch. In her previous life, competing with her twenty-three siblings to get to the food bowl first and down it fast, she must have acquired some ingenuity. This could explain her inner marathoner spirit.

Mandy doesn't know she's handicapped any more than bi-pods, tri-pods, and dogs in wheelchairs do. She's most happy when held, especially under any willing chin, as she throws her head back in the crook of a neck, releasing contented snorts and sighs.

Mandy the lil Dolphin

Mandy & Nash in a chin cuddle

Another standout survivor and one-time houseguest was Winston, a small Chihuahua found foraging behind a garbage dumpster. Finding no identification or posted flyers nearby bearing his name under a "Lost Dog" headline, Carol rescued him. She was walking her dog at the same time and couldn't bear to leave him there all alone, so she drove him home to discuss options with her husband, Richard. They were planning to travel for two weeks and had a friend lined up for the care of their current dog. Feeling pressed for time and not completely prepared to acquire another dog, they delivered Winston to the local animal control shelter.

The next day, Richard had second thoughts. He couldn't stop thinking about Winston, and with Carol's agreement, he contacted the shelter to get him back.

During a complete vet exam, required as part of the county's intake process, Winston was diagnosed with a liver condition that would require lifelong medication. Undeterred by news of Winston's condition, this lovely couple proceeded with the adoption and contacted Doolittle's Doghouse for his pet-care needs while they traveled.

Winston arrived with a bevy of medications to be administered three times a day. Winston required an insipid liquid to be injected by mouth, and the poor pooch summarily spewed it, wishing to resist. You can relate if you've had to do the same, singing along with Mary Poppins's "Spoon Full of Sugar." Unfortunately, even the enthusiasm of Julie Andrews doesn't make it any tastier for the recipient.

I wanted to find a sugary way to dispense this particular medicine to keep Winston from making an association between being held in my arms and the negative consequence: *Bam! Taste this!* Since Winston may have been on the streets for an undetermined amount of time without human touch or affection, this was especially important.

I contacted their vet regarding another option: Can I put it in his food? After the vet confirmed the medicine's effectiveness would not be compromised, the syringe went into his wet Freshpet instead of his mouth. Hallelujah! He gobbled it with glee.

We now had a tasteful regime for Winston. Two weeks later, his family returned from vacation and arrived to fetch him. The reunion was joyful, complete with wagging tails and exhilaration. This dog had only known his new owners for a few days before they left him in my care; yet he knew he belonged to them.

I was twenty feet away, observing all this happiness, when Winston suddenly turned and trotted over to me as if to say, "Thank you. I had a good time here." It was such an overt gesture on his part that my tears welled and fell. Richard and Carol quickly consoled me and promised I could visit them anytime.

Winston the Street Survivor

Dogs deserve all the sweetness we have to offer; yet so often they handle bitter circumstances with resilience and instinctive survival skills. They don't complain, they mask their pain, and they still love us despite our human frailties.

Those rescuing a dog don't always get insight into prior ownership history or previous experiences. Even dogs with horrible pasts can reclaim their spirit and trust in us with proper patience and love.

The best example of this remarkable ability to turn tail is the outstanding work of Best Friends Animal Sanctuary in Utah. In 2008, twenty-two traumatized dogs arrived at the Sanctuary, rescued from the kennels of professional football player, Michael Vick. They'd suffered unfathomable abuse due to a pitiful owner who bred them to fight … each other.

These dogs are now referred to as the Vicktory Dogs, as they received boundless love and emotional support from the Sanctuary staff. All but two have been adopted by loving families. Some have actually become service or therapy dogs. You can read their stories at https:// bestfriends.org/stories-about-dogs.

Dogs that have been surrendered, abandoned, or abused do not give up on us humans, as demonstrated by their resilience and willingness to trust again. It's a win-win game.

CHAPTER TWENTY-TWO

RESCUE REMEDIES—PATIENCE, DEVOTION, AND POULTRY

As some dogs develop baggage due to an unknown or unfortunate past, it's often necessary to employ a professional dog trainer or canine behaviorist to help unpack the issues causing difficult behavior.

The most valuable training tool I have learned and continue to employ was offered by Kathrine Breeden, professional canine trainer at https://bekindtodogs.com. Given our shared belief in positive reward and force-free methods, I've found her "Treat and Retreat" tips to be immensely successful when working with behaviorally challenged dogs. Some dogs develop emotional distress, similar to the way humans develop PTSD, which requires a little finesse to address.

With a myriad of dog treats available, it's important to choose the "golden nuggets" that will have the tastiest and greatest impact. Kathrine's top pick is cooked skinless chicken cut in small chunks. She carries her pouch of poultry when greeting every new client.

The first thing she does is throw a fistful of chicken away from her and toward the dog without looking at them, fawning over them, or providing any interaction beyond "I bring food."

Typically, the dog will gobble up the scattered morsels and return for more. When they return, she tosses another round of chicken. This process is repeated until the dog is at her feet and eating out of her hand.

I like to refer to this training activity as the "food fling" method. I have used it often with amazing success. While I want to believe that all dogs will love me at first sight, some of them need more time to develop trust.

When we first meet for boarding evaluation, it's like a blind date—we need to get to know each other based on the dog's terms and her expectations. Those with emotional damage, due to bad owners or a tragic experience, are understandably more fearful and reluctant to approach.

Enter Cammie, a small Jack Russell Terrier-Chihuahua-Cocker mix. Helen called with her boarding request and explained that Cammie is afraid of people and will bark to express her reticence and insecurity. Helen had rescued Cammie from a shelter, and they have developed a wonderful bond in their two years together. Cammie was still a work in progress when it came to bonding with others.

Armed with this information, I invited Helen and Cammie to meet me and asked her to bring a bag of chicken or Cammie's favorite golden treats. I met them in the driveway and grabbed the bag from Helen as Cammie began barking at me. Three food fling sessions and fifteen minutes later, Cammie was eating out of my hand and happily trotted into my home.

As my son was home on college break at the time, it was necessary to introduce Cammie to him as well, employing the same methodology. At first sight of my son—who was only half awake from a cocooning nap—Cammie began nipping at his heels with serious barking to boot.

I quickly flung the food at Nash, instructing him to toss the food in her direction, as we all backed away. Three fistfuls later, they were best friends.

Following this second successful introduction, Nash invited a childhood friend to come over. I trusted that Sean could handle this assignment, as I have known his family for years; they are not only dog owners and dog lovers, but they're also the most laid-back family I know. I met Sean in the driveway to provide brief instructions and hand over the treats. Without hesitation or nervousness whatsoever, Sean followed the game plan, and Cammie performed as before. Her behavior was now consistent with two new strangers in the house she had accepted as safe.

We spent a wonderful weekend together. She followed us, her new human friends, everywhere—with food in tow, of course. She happily snuggled in our laps, slouched on the couch, and rolled over for frequent belly rubs.

She soon began showing guardianship of us with appropriate "alert" barking as she patrolled our backyard.

When Nash decided to host a bevy of friends later that week, we agreed they would entertain themselves on the outside patio, entering and exiting through a side gate, while Cammie and I stayed indoors. Despite the fact that his friends have grown up with us and are accustomed to seeing a different pack of dogs in our house at any given time, we didn't have enough chicken to go around, nor did I want to over-stimulate Cammie. This work-around played out just fine. Despite the revelry and activity outside, just us girls snuggled quietly on the other side of the sliding door.

Subsequent staycations in my home have been effortless. Cammie trots to my front door and enters silently, yet with a "smiling" tail swishing back and forth. We have bonded comfortably like a pair of old shoes.

After three of Cammie's blissful and harmonious stays, Helen had a trip planned that I could not accommodate, due to another guest in residence. As we didn't trust Cammie with other dogs, I recommended another nanny, Margaret, a wonderful widow without her own critters. Margaret was raised on a farm, has seen it all, and is unflappable—and she has a sixth sense with animals.

Their advance consultation went much the same as ours, except this one included Margaret's home-cooked chicken added to the offering. True to form and belly, within minutes of "treat and retreat," Cammie was eating out of Margaret's hand.

I'm convinced that through patience and continued practice with this unique cuisine routine, Cammie will eventually stop her fearful barking at strangers and find peace in the presence of other humans—with or without the chicken.

Cammie-my Food Fling Success Story

Cammie and Nash- bonded in Trust through Chicken

While Cammie responded quickly, another client Edison (aka, Eddie) took a little longer and required greater benefaction.

When hired to provide twice-daily potty-break visits for Eddie and his furry sibling, Lucy, I encountered extreme reluctance from this handsome Staffordshire-mix who had been rescued by his devoted dog mom, DeeDee. While I had met with DeeDee and her furry kids in advance, I arrived solo and armed with a tub of cooked chicken and hope—on a 107-degree Arizona summer day.

As I let myself into the home the first day, Lucy greeted me with goofy happiness while Eddie quickly retreated to a bedroom. Avoiding eye contact, I tossed a procession of chicken in his direction, paired with brief animated conversation. Lucy's affection and keen interest was comical as we skipped outside. Though we left a trail of food toward the open back door, Eddie was steadfast in his bedroom vigil; he did not accept my culinary invitation to join us during either pop-in that first day.

Our daily visits are booked in only one-hour increments, with shortened outdoor activity due to the threat of summer heatstroke, and given just two hours to make a connection, the first day was a bust. Imagine the bladder control of a dog too scared in the presence of a stranger to relieve himself.

Undeterred and determined, I returned the next day for a repeat performance. While Lucy patrolled outdoors, I sat patiently in an Adirondack chair under the shade of a tree with my head down, using my iPhone camera as my "eye" on the scene while silently praying.

As Eddie slowly advanced from his bedroom retreat and sauntered outside to conduct his business, with only a cautious glance in my direction, I celebrated.

This same solemn ritual ensued all week, with only moderate success as Eddie would make an outdoor appearance, staying a little longer each time and eventually getting closer to me, yet not exactly eating out of my hand. He continued to harbor from a safe distance. The last day, he actually stayed outdoors to romp with Lucy and engage in "patio patrol" for an entire twenty-five minutes while I swatted mosquitos and remained rooted in my backyard nesting corner so as not to disturb his moment of serenity. We gained ground that week from complete retreat from me to a "safe" distance within three feet of each other.

While it was a relatively peaceful way to coexist in these brief intervals together in five short days, and only ten hours total, I firmly believe that given more time, if not cooler weather to linger longer, we can narrow the spatial distance drawn between us.

I cannot guarantee that this seemingly simple offer of friendship through food will work with every dog who suffers from understand-able hostility or fear. Depending on the dog's individual disposition, you may need to experiment with different methods before discovering the ideal way to a dog's heart. There's no one-size-fits-all training technique to earn their trust.

An important lesson to be learned from Cammie and Eddie: don't expect overnight success with your newly rescued dog. Be patient and tolerant, and do not hesitate to seek professional assistance to help forge a bond between you and your dog.

Dogs that have suffered abuse or landed in shelters are understandably freaked out, marinating on the inequities of their experiences and whatever circumstances landed them in their temporary, homeless condition. "Pound hounds" are surrounded by other insecure and equally scared cellmates, *not one of which* deserves to be in that scary place.

With Godly patience and realistic expectations, we are all capable of drawing back the veil and discovering the charm that lives inside each dog.

Treat and Retreat

Kathrine Breeden
www.bekindtodogs.com
kathrine@bekindtodogs.com
480.272.8816

This handout covers the basic procedure for "Treat and Retreat" with fearful dogs.

The process involves the dog approaching the scary human in her own time at her own speed.

Provide a bowl of fresh water where the dog feels safe to get it.

The human is seated or standing and remains in the same place throughout the session. The dog is allowed to approach or even just look at the human who tosses a treat or treats BEHIND the dog.

The dog is allowed to go and get the treat and then has the choice to approach the human again.

The human should not make any eye contact or talk to the dog or in any way attempt to engage the dog.

The dog will gradually get closer and closer to the human who should continue to toss the treats away from the dog.

That is the "treat" and the "retreat".

Watching the dog's body language closely will indicate how she is feeling about the human. It's always best to err on the side of caution and avoid forcing any contact on the fearful dog. Only when you are certain that the dog is comfortable and is soliciting, and is comfortable with attention, can the human try a little eye contact or speak in a quiet gentle voice to the dog.

If the dog starts barking or any sign of distress with eye contact, however brief, is made, go back to the beginning and start over.

Short & sweet is the motto. Numerous short successful sessions will work much better than long sessions. Try to always end on a good note.

<u>Do NOT let dogs who are fearful of strangers see the stranger leave.</u> Put the dog in another room while the visitor leaves. We want the dog to be disappointed when they return to the room and find the treat dispensing human has left.

©2018 Be Kind To Dogs Kathrine Breeden.

CHAPTER TWENTY-THREE
NATURE, NURTURE, AND THE UNKNOWN

Careless breeding is an unfortunate occurrence that may result in an unhealthy dog. Intact males and non-spayed females too often create accidental litters. Backyard breeders, hoping to make a buck, may not have the breed preservation as a priority, and in some cases, professional breeders may not be aware of a genetic defect in the parents.

Fortunately, there are many reputable breeders who are committed to the integrity of the breed line and follow strict guidelines in properly rearing pups for our companionship.

If you are considering a puppy purchase, following a thorough review of specific breed characteristics that match your family lifestyle, your next step is to find a reputable breeder. You might begin your research with a visit to the AKC website.

To ensure you receive the bang for the bigger bucks you shell out for a purebred dog, review the breeder's credentials, years of experience, and affiliations with breed clubs. You should also expect to receive documentation of the pup's pedigree, AKC registration, the breeder's guarantee of health, and vaccinations performed.

Ask your breeder if they sell to stores and if they are willing to give you the name of their veterinarian (so you can call their vet to "vet" details regarding the breeder's reputation and the health of their dogs). If you get a yes to the first question and a no to the second, proceed with caution.

Be sure to ask for other references along with their protocols for socializing the puppies from birth to your acquisition; you want to be sure they are interacting with other dogs, humans, and environmental landscapes beyond their pen.

A good breeder should be asking YOU questions about your home environment and family dynamics to determine compatibility. If possible, arrange to visit the breeder's home and spend time with the litter and the pup's parents.

Each puppy is a little snowflake with his own unique personality traits independent of breed characteristics.

As you observe litter interaction, ask the breeder to describe each pup. Expect descriptions like *athletic, the runt, boisterous, curious,* or *calm.* It's okay to ask for clarification: "What do you mean by athletic?" Hint: your ideal dog may be an aspiring Olympian vaulter, but you're looking at a Bassett Hound.

Bassett Hounds are built for endurance over speed, and they move deliberately not demonstrably. As scent hounds, they are more likely to have their noses to the ground, and at a maximum height of fourteen inches, they're unable to achieve great heights, such as your kitchen counter, despite best efforts or desire.

Meet the dog's parents too. I sadly recall a client with a genetically challenged Dane. While engaging with the breeder, blissfully preparing to drive her new puppy home, she disregarded the behavior of the pup's mom, who promptly bit her in the behind upon introduction. This real-life story did not end well.

CHAPTER TWENTY-FOUR
CAN I SEE YOUR DOG'S ID?

Regrettably, shelter dogs arrive in their unfortunate station for a variety of reasons. Many of them simply got loose and are never returned home due to improper identification. Good Samaritans who happen on a lost dog will first check for tags, might visit a local vet's office in the hope the dog is microchipped, or circulate flyers to post "Found Dog," which is hit-and-miss depending on how far that dog has traveled on his own. Sadly, when the owner can't be located, the dog becomes inadvertently and unfortunately homeless.

It's mind-boggling to me that any dog might be running loose without proper identification, which severely limits their ability to return home safely. If you've overlooked the importance of tagging your dog, please visit any large pet store or Walmart location for a cheap ID tag, and remember to update them when your address or phone number changes.

A safer bet to wage against the gamble of irretrievably losing your dog is to microchip him. Many local chapters of the Humane Society and ASPCA offer free microchipping. This *free service is offered to reduce the amount of shelter intake.* Your veterinarian may also offer this service along with their advice regarding the pros and cons.

If you haven't "tattooed" your dog and are curious about the procedure, editors for Petco offer this dogma on microchipping:

> A microchip is a radio-frequency identification device about the size of a grain of rice. These tiny devices contain an identification number that is unique to your pet and tied to an online database with your contact information.

When a special scanner is waved over the microchip, it reads the chip's frequency and displays the identification number. Typically, a veterinarian's office, animal shelter or law enforcement agency has a handheld scanner to use for this purpose.

When the number is entered into the online database, the person who scanned the chip can retrieve contact information and reunite the pet with his family.

According to the American Veterinary Medical Association, microchips only contain an ID number. The chip itself does not contain any contact information **[nor can it track a pet]**. When you register your pet in the database, you can provide additional pet information if you choose.

The chip process is quick and usually painless. Using a hypodermic needle, microchips are implanted between the shoulder blades under the animal's skin. General anesthesia is not necessary, though local anesthesia may be used.

Within 24 hours, the pet's tissue usually bond to the chip so it stays in place. (In rare instances, the chip can migrate to another part of the pet's body. The microchip can still be detected if the person performing the scan passes over another area of the body.) Allow the microchip insertion site to fully heal before bathing or grooming your pet.[18]

Lastly, it's important to keep your pet's microchip information and dog tags up to date if you relocate—easy to forget yet easy to do.

Most of our pet parents have microchipped their dogs and I have yet to hear of any negative consequences as a result.

---

18   "What You Should Know about Microchipping," Doolittle's Doghouse, accessed December 3, 2018, https://doolittlesdoghouse.com/what-you-should-know-about-microchipping/.

If any of these details have you feeling squeamish or uncertain about microchipping your dog, you might also consider outfitting your dog with a pet-tracking device in addition to microchipping. As an affiliate marketer of products with panache, we recommend the **GPS Whistle Tracker**. This tracking device combines cellular and GPS technology, attaches to your dog's collar, and can track a loose dog up to 3,000 miles away. Built-in location alerts will immediately notify you when your dog has left the building. You can also measure your dog's daily activity levels and set new goals for her fitness program. This is a valuable tool for any dog owner, especially those who own Houdini types known for their escape artistry skills.

CHAPTER TWENTY-FIVE
SENIOR CANINE CITIZENS

Every dog requires our daily attention and diligent protection, but elderly dogs with age-related conditions require extra special care. As they begin to slow down in life, our concerns take on a deeper and more meaningful level of commitment.

Cleopatra was a queen in her own right, introduced to me from day one as a dog with degenerative eye disease. She had just enough peripheral vision to still see shadows and images. In no way was this little Shih Tzu impaired by her disability.

Despite her diminished eyesight, she hung with the best of them. She was included in our daily walks, easily navigating up and down curbs or changes of terrain from grass, flattened earth, or uneven concrete to keep in perfect step with the other dogs. She could internally calculate the distance and location of available space on the dog-sanctioned futon to successfully make the launch. She was unperturbed by other dogs. And, at the age of thirteen, she was not prone to play yet quite content in her surroundings.

Eventually, however, her eyesight gave out completely. Where she was once familiar with my home environment, she began bumping into furniture and getting lost while on a stroll in the backyard. She would suddenly stop in her tracks, frozen in her uncertainty. I would quickly scoop her up and hold her in my arms to reassure her that she wasn't lost and alone in her now-dark world. I rearranged the furniture when she came to board.

From that sightless point forward, she spent most of the time in my lap or sleeping on her bed. Cleopatra never complained, whimpered, or showed any signs of distress. She was healthy in every other way and seemed to accept her circumstances while relying on her remaining senses, heightened by necessity.

Cleopatra-the Sightless Queen

I am especially moved by Cleopatra's graceful endurance of her elderly life progressions. By contrast, I steadfastly refuse to purchase dime-store readers and will continue to squint to see the fine print due to my own vanity, which is devoid of a dog's natural and passive acceptance.

It's paramount as a pet parent to make personal sacrifices for aging dogs when they've still got their joie de vivre. Life-threatening illnesses are always challenging, yet most senior conditions are easily managed.

Casper was my friendly ghost inside a gray Miniature Schnauzer; we first met when he was fourteen. He was that special senior dog whose movements were hardly noticeable, much like the quiet and friendly apparition who was his namesake. This special dog didn't require active boarding; he just needed a safe place to eat and sleep. His head was in a permanent cockeyed position due to a stroke.

When he did rise to the occasion, he didn't give any notice that it was time to "go"; he would stand and pee wherever he was. This never got a rise out of me, as I fully understood his lack of mobility and his frailty. More important to me was making provision for his comfort.

I had other choices, of course, none of which was to decline Casper's boarding needs, despite his declining health. I could have put him in diapers. Some dogs require daily diapering due to incontinence or chronic marking. It all Depends.

For Casper, diapers weren't necessary; we got outside often enough to mitigate the occasional mopping of the floor when I couldn't move fast enough or was working upstairs and didn't hear his quiet movements below when it was time to go.

As a dog owner and canine caretaker, you just have to be there for them. It flows both ways and is unconditional. I've met many senior dogs who defied their years and continued to romp with delight. Their company has provided not only personal entertainment and joy, but their very presence brings hope to the rest of us that the best is yet to come.

Betsy, a fifteen-year-old Bichon and contented lounge lizard at home, showed her I've-still-got-it strut when she came to stay with my bevy of boarders. When we saddled up for a walk, Betsy included, she lost all senior demeanor, with such enthusiasm and renewed spring in her step that even I was amazed.

We were careful to ensure she didn't tire quickly or stumble while navigating our neighborhood curbs and curves, and she never hesitated for a moment in that half mile. I'm not certain if her unexpected exuberance was due to the stimulation from a change of scenery or if it was simply the result of peer pressure.

To put this in perspective, *a dog at the age of six is akin to a forty-five-year-old human. At ten, they're almost sixty-five; at twelve they're approaching seventy-five in human years; and at fifteen they're rivaling a ninety-year-old.*

Consider how old your dog is in order to prepare for life changes ahead. It's important to keep your senior dog active with moderate exercise, continued daily mental enrichment, and life-stage nutritional adjustments.

Senior dogs require a diet that is 30–40% fewer calories, high in fiber, and low in fat, and should include vitamin and joint supplements. While older dogs require protein to maintain muscle mass, many "senior dog" foods have reduced levels of protein. It is a misconception that protein will enhance or promote renal failure in older dogs. A senior dog's diet should contain high-grade, digestible proteins in order to maintain muscle mass and proper immune functions.

Subtle signs of change aren't always apparent to a parent, as your expectations and daily routines become your norm, and it's easy to miss what's happening under your nose.

I especially appreciate those pet parents who have adopted senior dogs, as they are frequently overlooked by shoppers at the shelters. They are the last to be adopted and the first to be euthanized. There are many advantages to acquiring an older dog, particularly if you are a little bit older and can't run as fast as you used to; chasing a puppy all day requires parents who can match their boundless energy.

A senior dog has been around the block and requires less training. They settle in quickly, are past their teething years, are less likely to chew on your personal possessions, and have reached their full size and developed personality, which is apparent up front. They are calmer and more focused and can still be taught new tricks.

If you aren't ready for a commitment spanning several years, yet desire canine companionship, an older dog can provide some of your best moments in life together. These animals have old-soul wisdom and lessons in love left to share.

CHAPTER TWENTY-SIX

CONDITIONS AND TREATMENTS FOR OLDER DOGS

Pets in advanced age experience the same aches, pains, and illnesses humans' experience—from arthritis to zinc poisoning, and everything in between. What can you do as a devoted pet parent to ensure the continued health and vitality of your furry loved ones?

Medically speaking, the first answer is to *schedule semiannual well exams* with your family veterinarian. It's important to build a close relationship with him or her to ensure an open and honest line of communication. This is especially vital when it comes to a noticeable change in your pet's behavior requiring you to consult with a professional about your observations and concerns.

As dogs and cats are very good at masking their pain, only you know when something is wrong that demands professional attention. I hear too many stories about pet parents who avoid contacting their veterinarian due to the possible cost involved. We seek advice on the Internet instead.

A quick Google search might help you find short answers to a question, but it can't effectively identify specific issues or symptoms that only a qualified veterinarian can address. In order to be prepared for advanced age-related afflictions, review this condensed list of common senior conditions and suggested treatments.

Arthritis and Joint Pain:

If your dog isn't climbing the stairs, isn't walking as far as usual, has trouble getting up or down, or slips on slick floor surfaces, anti-inflammatories and/or joint supplements can help.

Consider slip-proofing your floors and provide soft beds for slumber.

For calloused elbows, open a vitamin E capsule and apply the oil to the sore areas. Cut the toes off a sock and slide it onto the anointed area to avoid licking.

Lightly massage your dog.

Exercise is still important for helping your senior dog maintain a healthy body weight. Overweight dogs suffer from a number of health problems beyond their climbing years.

Even though their metabolism is naturally slowing down, that doesn't mean you stop walking them. Simply shorten the time and distance, while keeping them on the move. Consider swimming as a means of low-impact exercise; it will put less stress on older and less nimble joints. Invest in a floatation vest for added security and ease of movement.

Dental Disease:

It's reported that 20% of dogs develop some form of dental disease *by the age of five.*

Bad breath or stained teeth is the first clue. If your dog has bad breath, it's because of bad teeth or plaque buildup. *Something else to chew on:* if untreated, this can lead to decay, tooth loss, and possible infection.

An owner shared with us the story of her six-year-old Doberman,

Eli, who was given a curious diagnosis of CUPS, a mouth disease that causes painful ulcers on the gums and mouth lining.

The cause of CUPS is a hypersensitive immune response to bacteria and plaque on the tooth surfaces. Fortunately for Eli, Mom caught it early, so only a few teeth had to be pulled. Had it gone untreated, he would have lost all his teeth.

Actively brushing their teeth, providing hard-surface chew toys or bones, and periodically taking them for professional cleanings are recommended treatments. Whiffing those not-so-heavenly fumes when you get nose to nose with your pet can be easily remedied.

Heart Disease:

Heart valve digression might lead to enlargement of the heart and possible failure. Early diagnosis is critical. If you notice your dog having difficulty breathing or tiring quickly during a walk, call your vet and schedule an X-ray.

I failed to insist on an X-ray during a well exam following these signs with my beloved Nikki. She was frequently collapsing while on a walk; her back legs would give out as if they had turned to rubber. She tired quickly from a short jaunt down a sidewalk. Sadly, she passed from congestive heart failure, but had her condition been properly diagnosed and treated with medication, we would have had more time to stroll through life together.

Heart disease can be treated with a low-salt diet, minimized exercise, and medication to boost heart function. While this condition will require that you keep your dog from over-exertion, you can still provide super low-impact activities for entertainment and stimulation. Toy puzzles are fun for every dog and might be a good way to keep your senior dog in heart-healthy and active condition.

Diabetes:

Increased thirst and urination, weight loss, unusually sweet-smelling breath, dehydration (evidenced by sticky gums), chronic skin infections, urinary tract infections, or lethargy are signs of diabetes. With early diagnosis, this is treatable with medications, a high-fiber diet, and in most cases, insulin injections.

Canine Cognitive Dysfunction:

Akin to Alzheimer's in humans, this is a decline in the mental faculties. Be aware that *50% of dogs over age ten will exhibit one or more symptoms of cognitive dysfunction syndrome.*

Symptoms might include disorientation, sleep interruption, aimless wandering, and indiscriminate elimination. Behavioral changes, such as needing more attention or no attention at all, could mean your dog is reacting to his own symptoms and uncertainty.

Have you ever walked into a room and paused to wonder, *why did I come in here?* If you can relate and notice your dog experiencing these common "senior moments," consult with your vet to rule out other possible conditions.

Changing your dog's diet to include omega-3 fatty acids and antioxidants may help slow the progression. Updating your dog's routines by adding mental enrichment games, toys, and new activities such as a foray to a park you haven't visited or varying your walking routes can help stimulate his brain.

Hearing loss:

As dogs age, the nerve cells degenerate, resulting in a slow loss of hearing. This is not normally a big deal, as we know that dogs read our body language and follow hand signals quite well.

Your smell and vibrations from your movements will help them find you. While we can't rewind the clock on their hearing, you can continue to enjoy an active lifestyle with your hearing-impaired dog. Just don't sneak up on them, or you might invite a bite!

Incontinence:

Loss of kidney function and urinary control may occur over time. Some of us have experienced a little piddle when we giggle. It may not be a laughing matter, yet uncontrollable release happens.

Medications can help mitigate incontinence. Doggie diapers or alternative treatment options may be considered also.

Eye disorders:

The most prevalent eye disorder in dogs is cataracts. While some breeds are genetically prone to cataracts, old age is the biggest factor. This is a progressive disorder that could lead to complete blindness. Your vet may recommend surgery or an alternative treatment, such as phacoemulsification.

Veterinary ophthalmology is beyond the scope of this book and is only mentioned here to provide a little insight. Treatment options might be available in cases of early diagnosis.

Tips for living with a sight-challenged dog are provided by Blind Dog Rescue Alliance (BDRA). This is a heralded group of volunteers dedicated to rescuing blind and visually impaired dogs. They will unequivocally testify to each volunteer's personal and spiritual growth, embracing human frailty through the teachings of each special-needs dog they have saved. Their mettle is fueled by the witness that "Blind dogs see with their hearts." In the many years that the Blind Dog Rescue Alliance has existed, they've saved over 500 sight-impaired dogs from shelters.

Blind Dog Rescue Alliance

Blind Dogs See With Their Hearts!

www.blinddogrescue.com

LIVING WITH A BLIND DOG

Did you know a dog's primary sense is smell, followed by hearing? Vision is a dog's third most important sense—that's relatively low on the list. Dogs also possess a skill called cognitive mapping. It's the same instinct that allows them to find an object they buried weeks ago. That's really handy for blind dogs. That's what enables them to "map" the house and yard. Here is a list of suggestions to help your blind dog live a normal life:

1. Try not to move furniture around or leave obstacles on the floor.

2. Ask people to let your dog "smell" their hand before touching them. Most blind dogs' personalities don't change. Some dogs however can easily become "startled" and this could lead to fear biting in some dogs.

3. Be creative with different scents to mark areas for your blind dog. Use different scents of flavored extracts or even something as simple as hanging a car air freshener or potpourri sachet on a door. Different scented candles in each room may also help your dog distinguish different rooms in the house. A dab of vanilla extract on the dog's sleeping spot, a touch of Pledge near the food bowl, and a drop of perfume near the door outside helps identify those key areas. Don't worry about whether you can smell the scent—your dog's nose is much more sensitive.

4. Use textured materials to mark areas. Throw rugs or carpet sample squares in doorways going into each room makes it easier to find the door openings. Wind chimes near the back door or dog door, or door mats at outside door entrances can be helpful to your dog getting headed back and in the door after going outside.

5. Use bells or jingling tags on your other dogs, not only to help your blind dog find/follow your other dogs, but also to avoid them being startled by your other dogs. You can also use bells on your shoes to help them find you.

6. Don't be afraid to walk with a "heavy foot" when approaching them especially with a blind/deaf dog...they can still feel vibrations.

7. Training is vitally important for blind dogs. Instead of just heel, sit and stay, owners need to add commands like "step up," "step down," "slow down," and "stop". This not only helps them to find you, but you can help them avoid obstacles. As you walk, apply a little backward pressure on the collar, or touch the dog's chest to slow it down, as you voice the word "easy" or "slow." Draw the word out so it sounds the way you want the dog to act—eeeaas-sssyyy. As the dog slows, feed it a treat.

8. A tabletop fountain can be used as a water bowl. Get a simple one with a large bowl. The sound of running water helps to orient the blind dog and find the water bowl as well as know where he is from the sound. Some dogs like drinking from running water too! This can be especially helpful if you have to move to a new home with a blind dog.

9. If your dog uses a crate - turn it on its side, so the door opens "up" and you can bungee the door in place. This way your dog doesn't need to worry that the door may only be partially open.

10. If you have young children that need to understand things are "new" for their doggie, have them put on a blindfold and crawl around so they can *see* that things are different for their pal.

11. Hearing your voice is very soothing, so talk to your blind dog often. Let them know when you are walking out of a room, etc. Even just some "silly chatter" is enjoyable to them, and really is kind of fun!

12. Remember to speak to your dog when you are approaching to touch (especially while sleeping) to prevent startling them.

13. If your dog wore a collar for walking before, now is a good time to try a harness. You have more control if the dog balks, with less stress to the neck and eyes, this is important with glaucoma.

14. Use a baby gate or a decorative fireplace screen to block stairs until your dog has mastered them. Teach stairs by placing a "treat" on every step or two. Stand in front of your dog, holding collar or harness, and gently encourage (without pulling). Practice until they are able to go up and down smoothly.

15. If boarding your dog, or leaving with the vet or groomer, make a special sign to have added to their kennel saying "I'm blind" to make sure all caregivers "know" your dog is blind.

16. Socialize your blind dog. Don't coddle them by picking them up to get to their food, water, or outside. Treat them as a regular dog and let them figure it out. Above all, be patient. Dogs can sense when you are frustrated or upset.

17. Finally, remember, blind dogs can live healthy, happy lives.

CHAPTER TWENTY-SEVEN
MEDICAL ADVANCEMENTS AND TREATMENT ALTERNATIVES

If you are paying attention to a change in your dog's condition, and hopefully scheduling *frequent well exams* with your vet, it's likely that routine changes in your dog will only require short-term remediation. In the alternative, you need to be prepared for other professional recommendations. Fido needs surgery. Fido has a condition that requires long-term medication or regularly scheduled injections. Now what?

Here's the good news: Veterinary treatment has progressed light years with several non-invasive alternatives for many "human" conditions diagnosed in our pets. Unique advancements with promising results include acupuncture, laser therapy, and hydrotherapy, as well as hemp-based (CBD) products.

Old dog, new prick? Acupuncture is gaining ground in the interest of alternative therapy for many conditions that may affect your dog and cat. While this is a sticky point, with some debate between traditional and holistic practitioners, acupressure and acupuncture might be a treatment to consider, particularly for pain management and temporary relief for your pets. Acupuncture in general is a 2,000-year-old Chinese practice rooted in the body's natural ability to self-heal.

According to Patrick Mahaney, VMD, Holistic House-Call Veterinarian and Certified Veterinary Acupuncturist (CVA):

> The goal of acupuncture is to promote the body to heal itself. From a Traditional Chinese Veterinary Medicine (TCVM) perspective, veterinary acupuncture encourages healing by correcting energy

imbalances in the body. Acupuncture enhances blood circulation, nervous system stimulation, and the release of anti-inflammatory and pain-relieving hormones.[19]

These alternative options include the use of lasers (needle-less treatments), aqua acupuncture (includes medicinal herbs or vitamins in the injections), moxibustion (Chinese herbal compounds are applied to the needles to provide added heat), and electroacupuncture (electrodes are attached to the needles for a mild, steady electric current to stimulate damaged nerves).

Both cats and dogs may benefit from acupuncture to treat a variety of ailments such as:

- Sore muscles and joints
- Arthritis
- Muscle spasms
- Degenerative joint disease
- Paralysis
- Digestive issues
- Cushing's disease (dogs)
- Hypothyroidism (dogs)
- Diabetes
- Heart disease
- Kidney disease
- Liver disease
- Ruptured discs
- Cancer

---

19   Patrick Mahaney, VMD, "Getting to the Point with Needles and Other Veterinary Acupuncture Treatments," PetMD, accessed December 4, 2018, https://www.petmd.com/dog/wellness/evr_multi_veterinary-acupuncture-for-dogs-cats.

- Dermatologic conditions, including allergic dermatitis and lick granulomas
- Asthma and other respiratory problems
- Epilepsy and seizures
- Weakened immune system

In 2015 the American Animal Hospital Association (AAHA) and American Association of Feline Practitioners (AAFP) issued joint guidelines that labeled acupuncture a "compelling and safe method for pain management" that "should be strongly considered" as part of a pain management plan in pets.

Acupuncture may also be combined with chiropractic care, massage therapy, aquatic fitness, physical therapy, and nutritional counseling. The decision to implement new treatments should not be taken "Cavalier-ly," instead they should be researched carefully in conjunction with consulting your family veterinarian, your pet insurance plan, budget, and your feelings about what is best for your pet.

Hemp products, with cannabinoid properties, are also growing in popularity as fast as weeds after a good rain. CBD, a cannabis extract, is cropping up as an optional treatment for dogs and cats suffering from a variety of ailments including anxiety, seizures, cancer, arthritis, joint inflammation, or general pain.

While hemp and marijuana are cultivated from the cannabis plant, the two main extracts, tetrahydrocannabinol (THC) and cannabidiol (CBD) are completely separate compounds with divergent medicinal applications and legal classifications. TCH is the psychoactive component of marijuana and largely recognized as producing a high. CBD, by itself, lacks the euphoric instigator of THC and is available over the counter and does not require card-carrying status to purchase.

I was inadvertently turned on to the benefits of Canna-Pet® nutritional hemp products by a good client whose five-year-old German Shepherd-Akita mix, Oakley, had suddenly developed a seizure disorder.

When Brian asked me to recommend a veterinarian, I sent him to a DVM I admire for his state-of-the-art clinic and vast years of experience. Following a thorough examination, Oakley was prescribed Keppra (an antiepileptic drug) for a few days then transitioned to a less-expensive, albeit experimental, treatment alternative: Canna-Pet® Canna-Biscuits for dogs, made with CBD from hemp.

As Oakley was not an overly problematic epileptic and had no prior history of seizures, he made a relatively safe transition from Keppra to cannabis. Within days of his twice-daily biscuit consumption, Oakley's seizures stopped completely, and he has been stable since.

I can personally testify to his renewed sense of balance as we were hired to walk Oakley every day following the arrival of a new baby. Brian and his wife, Grace, brought their newborn, Ella, home from the hospital and wanted to ensure that Oakley's routines were maintained, as they anticipated their lifestyle changes with an infant in the home.

Doolittle's nannies have provided for Oakley's morning strolls and in-home boarding needs since Ella's birth. Since providing consistent pet care during the past year, we confidently report that Oakley is trotting with no subsequent seizure episodes and continues to munch his Canna-Pet® biscuits without any noticeable side effects. The keen intelligence of this German Shepherd is an engaging demonstration of genetic instinct. He is on a *mission* during his daily walks with an exact idea of where he wants to go, which varies according to his choice.

His eyes and ears are in tune with any neighborhood activity several yards ahead of our footfalls; if I slightly inhale, no louder than a whisper, he glances back to check on me. He will park his nose intently on an obscure spot with a focus worthy of Sherlock Holmes. I can easily understand why this breed is so prominently favored for guide and guard dog service in airports, search and rescue, disability assistance, and as police and military partners.

Oakley with his Dad (Brian) and Sister (Ella)

Emmett, a darling Yorkshire Terrier who suffers from compromised joints (patellar luxation) is another canine acquaintance of mine who benefits from canna cookies, which he takes to remedy his periodic pain and lameness. This terminally cute dog has a little bit of everything going on. He has chronic wheezing and must don doggie diapers while indoors as he is a prolific marker. He just can't help himself, and we can't help but love him in spite of the myriad maladies in his tiny body.

The Yorkie originated in Yorkshire, England, in the 1900s to catch rats in clothing mills. They can be feisty and a bit bossy despite their average weight of only 7 pounds. These tiny pints have big-dog attitudes combined with entertaining personalities. They defy their diminutive stature and are extremely brave, loyal, and clever animals.

Emmett lives with a large, slow-lumbering 70-pound Lab (aptly named Moose) with steely resolve to rule the roost. Moose patiently ignores Emmett's periodic moments to prove, "I'm the boss around here." These brief demonstrations remind me of a schoolmarm with a ruler in hand, giving a quick shake of the stick to any defiant student who needs reminding that she's in charge. Emmett's version is to dart into Moose's face with a quick (fake) head butt to prove hierarchy.

Yorkies are prone to bronchitis (hence the heavy breathing) and rank in today's top 10 most popular breeds (according to the AKC and every Yorkie owner in the US).

Melissa, Emmett's mom, and I met two years ago when Emmett was only seven. Sadly, in this short time, Emmett's mobility has declined. His movement and breathing are strained, and he limps more frequently—usually following a high jump onto furniture. Emmett was prescribed Canna-Pet® for his joint pain and inflammation. He regained some motility, following a few months of hemp-packed biscuit consumption, if not a more mellow approach to his athletic aspirations.

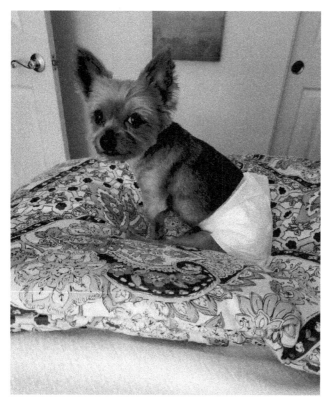

Emmett the diapered Yorkie

The veterinarian who recommends Canna-Pet® biscuits and capsules has reported overwhelmingly positive results in many of his clients. Personally, I would love to see any high-anxiety dog on Prozac try this instead. We have those clients too.

As other treatment methods are expensive, enrolling in a pet insurance plan may be a prudent consideration as well. Having the peace of mind that your pet is covered for potential illnesses and rehabilitation regimens might be worth the evaluation of individual plans and costs.

Megan, the devoted and loving owner of Henry, a spirited and engaging French Bulldog, will tell you that she choked on the monthly insurance premiums with some resentment, until Henry wrenched his back and required physical therapy. He's only five and a half years old. This little doggie is a Billy goat in disguise. He loves to climb to the top of furniture (his "mountains") and rest precariously on the headboards. His eyes light up at the sight of a toy box. Rather than carefully select one toy at a time, he will gleefully leap into the middle of the box to surround himself with every plush, rubberized, and squeaky *objets de désir* to find the right one then shake it to oblivion.

It's possible that one wrong shake of the head caused a spinal rift that now requires physical therapy with a veterinarian certified in acupuncture and water therapy. Fortunately for Henry, he is improving with these specialized treatments, and the majority of his medical expenses are covered by Megan's pet insurance plan.

The French Bulldog's origin began in the 1800s when bred with Bulldogs in England and Ratters from Paris with trademark "bat ears" and comical dispositions blended in the mix. Their vivacious and affectionate nature is captivating and, despite their clown-like antics, they are not prone to vocalization—an added bonus, especially for apartment-dwelling owners.

Despite the possibility of future illnesses or unexpected medical conditions, the average owner will routinely visit their veterinarian to maintain vaccination protocols. As we require shot records for every dog we board, it didn't take long to notice that some were getting rabies and DHPP vaccinations annually, while other dogs of *the same age* were receiving these standard vaccinations every three years.

What I've surmised from this curious disparity is that it may not be necessary to vaccinate *annually*, past the age of two, and furthermore possibly *discontinuing* Parvo/Distemper/Canine Hepatitis/Adenovirus (DAHP) past the age of ten.

Parvo-Distemper is a valid risk and fatal disease for puppies. Subsequently, this particular vaccination is often administered in the first four to six months of life. Hopefully, the puppy is off to a good start in developing a healthy immune system from the antibodies in their mother's milk. Once the puppy is weaned from Mom, the typical protocol is a series of three DAHP injections spaced two to four weeks apart and completed ideally by four months of age. It stands to reason that a ten-year-old dog should be relatively invulnerable.

Additionally, by the time your dog reaches two years of age, three-year boosters may be sufficient (as opposed to annual) for the core vaccinations mentioned above.

Frequency of rabies vaccinations are, of course, dictated by local regulations with individual state requirements. There are many other non-core vaccinations available, based on your dog's lifestyle and the environmental factors that may or may not pose risk to illness or disease. Some examples of optional vaccinations include Bordetella and Leptospira; whether these optional vaccines are applicable to your dog is a topic best raised with your veterinarian.

According to the American Veterinary Medical Association (AVMA) website, regarding the frequency of vaccinations:

> Many vaccinations provide adequate immunity when administered every few years, while others require more frequent schedules to maintain an acceptable level of immunity that will continually protect your pet.[20]

The AVMA recommends that veterinarians customize vaccination programs to the needs of their patients. More than one vaccination program may be effective.

---

20 "Vaccinations," AVMA, accessed December 4, 2018, https://www.avma.org/
public/PetCare/Pages/vaccinations.aspx.

A recent publication (2017) from the American Animal Hospital Association (AAHA) drills it down further.

> As Dr. Ronald Schultz, professor and chair of the department of pathobiological sciences at University of Wisconsin-Madison, states: "Be wise and immunize, but immunize wisely." Current (2011) American Animal Hospital Association (AAHA) recommendations for canine distemper and parvovirus vaccination are to vaccinate puppies at 12 and 16 weeks of age, booster at one year if the last puppy vaccine was at less than sixteen weeks of age, then re-vaccinate greater than or equal to every three years. However, the AAHA then goes on to say that the efficacy of the vaccines is at least five years:
>
> - "Among healthy dogs, all commercially available distemper vaccines are expected to induce a sustained protective immune response lasting at least five years."
>
> - "Among healthy dogs, all commercially available MLV-CPV-2 vaccines are expected to induce a sustained protective immune response lasting at least five years."[21]

Dogs with suppressed immune systems or existing health conditions require case-by-case consideration, wherein some or all vaccinations could be more harmful than beneficial.

In those rare cases that a dog shows a severe reaction to a routine vaccination or has immune-related diseases, a titer test can be performed instead. A titer test is a simple blood test used to measure a dog or cat's antibodies against vaccine virus or infectious agents, particularly with core diseases such as Canine Parvovirus, Canine Distemper, and Canine Hepatitis. There is no downside to a titer test, other than

---

21 Lea Stogdale, DVM, "Study of Canine Vaccine Antibody Responses," *Innovative Veterinary Care Journal*, February 3, 2017, https://ivcjournal.com/vaccine-antibody-responses/.

the vagaries of test result interpretation if the results are negative. A negative titer test does not immediately suggest that a dog is unprotected. It could simply reflect the fact that the titer has not yet reached an ideal antibody level to confidently measure.

While there may be some debate as to when and how often specific vaccinations should be administered, *routine health exams* should be maintained to proactively guard against other potential illnesses and health threats. Even the slightest change in your dog's demeanor deserves a veterinarian's attention.

Some indicators are hard to ignore. Teddy, a congenial and otherwise healthy one-year-old Bichon Frise suddenly lost all energy and appetite for food. His rapid weight loss and disinterest in playing ball or springing for a walk prompted a trip to the vet. Following requisite tests, he was diagnosed with Valley Fever. Karen, his mom, and her family veterinarian agreed to discontinue all other vaccinations while Teddy was on medication to treat Valley Fever.

Valley Fever is not life threatening and can affect both dogs and humans. It is not transmittable and is easily treated. It is a fungal disease contracted through infectious dust spores found in dry desert climates. These malevolent mold-like contagions lie dormant until a good rain. The spores then rise like an army of Darth in-Vaders and become airborne to be inadvertently inhaled, particularly by those dogs who like to sniff and dig in the dirt. It is not contagious, and healthy dogs that come into contact with these nasty desert "dwellers" may not ever contract the disease. Younger dogs, like Teddy, and those with suppressed immunity are more susceptible.

Brett the Vet suspended all other routine vaccinations in the interest of protecting Teddy's health during his recovery. This also required that Teddy not be boarded with other dogs, despite his social nature, playfulness, and ability to get along with other dogs—a trait the Bichon is well known for.

The Bichon Frise has an ancient, if not colorful past originating in the Mediterranean; crossed with a family of large water dogs (the Barbet) with small coated white ones, this new breed was known as Barbichons (later abbreviated to Bichon). Dating as far back as the 1400s, the Bichon Frise survived several invasions of conquering countries from Italy to France, landing in the laps of French kings. In the early nineteenth century, its popularity waned. Its place was no longer in palaces but more commonly with street performers. They became the proverbial "monkey" for organ grinders until French breeders elevated them to their deserved notoriety in 1933. Following World War II, they came to America, and with a redesigned coat, this wonderful companion animal captured hearts and a position with the AKC by 1971. Their magnificent coat, if groomed to breed standards, resembles a body of cumulous clouds. They are animated cotton balls with a jovial disposition.

Teddy the Bichon Frise

All things considered, and despite current or future afflictions both benign and injurious, from puppyhood to passing, dogs deserve a lifetime commitment from their caregivers—they're yours to have and to hold, in sickness and in health.

CHAPTER TWENTY-EIGHT

SOMETHING IN THE WAY YOU MOVE

Zoey, the Easter basket thief, was a regular guest for many years, despite her sneaky way with food and healthy appetite for any food item—including the most unimaginative produce. Her extremely gentle demeanor captured my heart at first sight.

When her mom, Phyllis, first called for pet care, we scheduled the requisite advance visit. I hadn't met a purebred Bull Mastiff yet, so I was curious to see how this 120-pound dog would behave, especially around smaller dogs.

Phyllis arrived in her Escalade (driving a Prius is not an option with this breed), and Zoey stepped onto my front lawn off leash. There was something in the way she moved that moved me. She had a slow and majestic manner, walking with patient deliberation toward the front door. That was all I needed to see; before I opened the door, I knew she was a keeper.

Zoey became a regular guest and was a huge delight to have around. While some big dogs think they are lapdogs, Zoey was acutely aware of her largeness. She knew she was bigger than the average dog and accepted that the smaller ones might not want to play with her as a result. Just about every dog in our home was smaller, so she was always a minority in the size department.

Zoey never showed any signs of frustration at this natural discrimination. She would patiently lay (actually sprawl) on her king-size pet bed, roll over for belly rubs at every opportunity, and in the morning before being let outside, would run to the food bowl in anticipation of breakfast. While most dogs need to be let outside first, Zoey operated in the reverse. Food was her solace.

She was astoundingly patient when bunking with other dogs. She reminded me of a prom girl who is the last one asked to dance. With complete acceptance and understanding, she would simply wait for an invitation to play and never provoked or prompted another dog to engage. However, when any dog would give the signal "I'm okay, you're okay, so let's play," she would spring from the ground and jitterbug with excitement.

The most amazing relationship existed between Zoey and the "Tiny Prancer" Maggie—120 pounds to Maggie's 5 pounds. Despite Maggie's diminutive size, she had no fear when Zoey was near.

I cannot explain why Maggie was untouched by trepidation. I imagine she simply sensed she was safe next to this massive yet gentle Mastiff.

Zoey & Maggie; best friends and BFF

Zoey's patience and premeditation would present itself later when food was involved. Her pet bed was the size of a small futon, which also served as her lair.

Phyllis warned me about Zoey's sneaky way of stealing food when no one is looking. She described an incident in her mother's home when the pantry door was inadvertently left open and Zoey scoured through a bag of flour. Can you picture a Bull Mastiff's face covered in white makeup? Not to mention the paw prints artfully painted upon the flour-coated floor.

All food in my home had to be stored safely behind locked doors and out of nose reach. Not one crumb on the counter was safe. While this is a common problem in most households, Zoey wasn't a counter surfer in the true sense. She would spot an ingestible object of desire and plot to obtain it when the time was right.

As Thanksgiving is followed so quickly by Christmas, I still had pumpkins and gourds decorating the front hallway, in addition to gift-wrapped bubble gum meant for my son's stocking. I'd thrown the sugar-free gum under the tree in haste as Zoey arrived for a Christmas stay.

After we unpacked her luggage, she went about her business and settled in, which included sniffing the holiday scenery. I'm sure she was thinking, *Gee, these are new.* Still, she didn't make a move (yet).

Several routine days followed with normalcy, until I left to run errands. This gave Zoey the perfect opportunity to satisfy her salivating curiosity. While I hadn't considered five small pieces of gum, wrapped twice, to be a "holiday hazard," Zoey proved me wrong.

Returning home, I found remnants of the wrappers scattered in her bed. It took a few minutes to assess this WTF moment. Realizing what had happened, I was thrown into a panic. Xylitol, a sugar-free substitute, is extremely toxic to dogs. I leapt to the phone to call Animal Poison Control to discuss the details and determine the level of threat to Zoey's health.

This service is staffed twenty-four hours a day by licensed veterinarians and toxicologists, and all calls are answered immediately. Much to my relief, given Zoey's body size versus the small amount of gum she consumed, I was assured she was safe from harm.

Three days later, I was on the phone with them again when Zoey consumed the small pumpkin on the floor, leaving only the stem and a few seeds as evidence. You would assume that I had removed any potential intestinal obstructions by now. Yet, who would have thought I needed to guard the gourds too?

Despite explaining for the second time in a week that I was the world's dumbest pet sitter, I was reassured that pumpkin—even without being pureed and with the rind intact—was a natural and harmless "appetizer." Zoey would be fine; there was no cause to worry.

Who's worried? This dog ate an entire Easter basket of chocolates in her own home. But this was on my watch; I was responsible for her safety.

Praise the Lord, I have not had to call ASPCA Animal Poison Control since. I hope you don't have to either. If you suspect your dog has consumed something harmful, do not hesitate to buzz your vet or the professionals on standby at 1-888-426-4435.

CHAPTER TWENTY-NINE
EARLY SOCIALIZATION IS FUNDAMENTAL

When Nikki, my Havanese, arrived as a delectable Christmas present, my son was four, and my Leonberger, Max, was at his top weight of 140 pounds. Nikki was ten weeks old and weighed less than ten pounds. This mold of "canine clay" grew up with a small child, a very big dog, and lots of other diverse playmates.

Due to early socialization with not only a big dog, but also those who came in and out like a Westminster parade, she had no fear or anxiety in a pack environment. This was her norm.

My fierce belief that no dog should be kept in a kennel or cage, nor isolated from family activities, including human kids and other critters, has allowed me to spin a small business for cage-free boarding. It's easy to connect the well-socialized dogs with one of my nannies—most of them own a dog or two, and a few own cats too. We pair our guests based on their size, age, disposition and, most importantly, their social skills—and whether they might chase the cats!

We do our best to board the dogs that cannot be around other dogs or animals due to a lack of sociability for whatever reason. Those who don't play well with others keep my pet-free nannies in high demand. It is critically important to include your dog in every aspect of your life and create a circus of positive stimulation as early and often as possible.

Dogs yearn to learn, relying on their innate abilities and senses, and they benefit greatly from interaction outside your home. Early and positive introduction to a variety of landscapes, people, kids, and other dogs and animals in public places helps develop their sense of social belonging and cooperation as a pack member.

Ideally, you want the confidence that your dog can successfully navigate new environments, especially when you plan a business trip or vacation that doesn't include them.

Dogs that are isolated develop many problems, including aggression, fear, or unusual shyness. They lack confidence when around new people or situations and may cower, pant excessively, drool, lower their tails, shake all over, attempt to escape the situation, or possibly growl and/or bite out of fear.

This important element of pet parenting is highlighted by Drs. Daniel Q. Estep and Suzanne Hetts, Certified Applied Animal Behaviorists. Hetts explains:

> Dogs have a sensitive period for socialization that occurs between the ages of three and twelve weeks of age. This means that pleasant exposure to people, other dogs, cats, and other animals … during this time will have long-lasting influences on the sociability of dogs.
>
> Puppies given these experiences during the sensitive socialization period tend to be friendlier and less fearful as adults … Don't underestimate how important it is to *continue to socialize your dog well into adulthood.* We've seen quite a few dogs who seem to have been well socialized early in life, were friendly and accepting of people and other dogs, and then began to react with threats or aggression during social encounters when they reached behavioral maturity. These dogs had no traumatic or frightening experiences but became fearful or aggressive beginning anywhere from eight months to around two years of age.[22]

---

22   Dr. Suzanne Hetts, "Why Socialization Isn't Just Important for Puppies," Behavior and Training Tips at SensibleDogTraining.com, audio, 00:27, http://sensibledogtraining.com/is-socialization-just-for-puppies/.

They cite their own experience with a certain client, Eddie. Eddie attended puppy classes and had frequent contact with people and dogs during puppyhood. He was a friendly guy. At the age of one and a half, his family moved from the city to the country, and Eddie saw very few people or animals in his new home. At the age of two, he began growling and lunging at people.

While the specific cause of Eddie's change in demeanor is unknown, it's worth considering that this sudden change of behavior might have been due to the absence of consistent social experiences.

Most of you are familiar with the marvelous Monks of New Skete, who for decades have bred and trained German Shepherds with unsurpassed success. They write in their book *How to Be Your Dog's Best Friend*:

> Dogs are social animals, and they need to be included in a pack. Since we have deprived them of their normal pack—animals of their own species—and the freedom to set up social structures of their own, we must include them in our pack and help them adapt to human social structures ... Many pet owners perceive their charges to be incapable of enjoying human company. The tendency is to isolate dogs rather than include them.[23]

The most painful experience I've had personally regarding the consequences of an isolated dog occurred with a young Havanese whose parents had little experience with pet ownership. I met them on the patio of a posh resort during a dog-friendly social affair and was naturally drawn to the furry cutie on her mom's lap.

As a fellow owner of a Havanese, I am acutely aware of this breed's marvelously social nature. The Havanese breed was introduced by Spanish traders as gifts to Cuban women, particularly the elite. Only

---

23   Monks of New Skete, *How to Be Your Dog's Best Friend* (Little, Brown, 2001).

a few were brought to the US in the fifties and sixties with increasing popularity since.

The "Havi" is extremely cordial and well known for its gregariousness with just about anybody, including animals, children, and other dogs. They are eager to please, and their happy nature shows in their gait, which resembles a bunny hop.

I'm drawn to any dog anywhere like a magnet, so I casually approached this couple with a fistful of business cards to tout Doolittle's Doghouse. While we were surrounded by several dogs and their owners, this one in particular was relegated to the laps of her parents and guarded zealously.

As if the mere suggestion that Fifi touch the cootie-laden concrete was out of the question, she never left the arms or lap of Mom and Dad the entire time we chatted and for the duration of this three-hour event.

I must have made an impression, as they called for pet care soon after. At first, Fifi was comfortable in my home, given another Havanese to play with. The adage "kissing cousins" is a real-life event with dogs of the same breed; they somehow know they share the same DNA and will typically and instantly bond like separated kin at a family reunion.

Over time, however, given the infrequency of visits and prolonged periods of isolation in her own home, unusual behaviors presented when Fifi arrived again for short stints. She became fearful of other dogs. She didn't like to go for walks and cowered in the corner for no reason. I knew the parents used a dog stroller, yet this wasn't an option in my home. We don't push our "babies" in their prams; we walk on all fours together to bond as a pack.

We cruise over grass, sidewalks, knolls, and rocks, and we stop to sniff or water every bush along the way. Whether squatting or lifting a leg, this is how dogs send messages to each other.

Fire hydrants, telephone poles, garbage receptacles, bushes, and other public objects subject to frequent marking are the most enjoyable sniffs for any dog … there's so much to read in the pee mail!

Sadly, Fifi didn't enjoy any of these normal dog behaviors. In talking to her parents, I garnered enough to know that she was not interacting with other dogs or people. She was guarded zealously in her own home, was rarely left alone, and was almost never taken out in public. I didn't know how to properly address this in our conversations, despite what I knew and should have said.

As Fifi's fear and paranoia of pets and people worsened, I could no longer accommodate her boarding needs. When I bumped into this family years later, Fifi was being strolled into a Pet Expo event in a baby carriage. She didn't recognize me and barked fitfully from the parking lot to the facility entrance. Despite her parents' best intentions, isolation had created an extremely frustrated dog.

Positive socialization can be easily accomplished with commitment and practice. Social activities can include attending dog obedience and agility classes, visiting dog-friendly stores and restaurants, and taking them with you in the car to visit friends and family—preferably those who own socially adapted dogs.

If you don't have a circle of canine-loving friends, jump on NextDoor. com, a free community chat room where you can connect with neighbors you haven't met yet who may be interested in swapping playdates or meeting in the park to play. Much like Facebook, although closer to home, you can simply post "looking for other dog owners to share walks and playtime together."

Meetup.com is another public forum to find pet-centric groups that meet regularly in public places with their dogs.

There are doggie day care facilities and training camps popping up on every corner. Your dog will need to pass a temperament test before enrolling in day care, but the group interaction can reap great rewards for your dog and is well worth the price of admission.

If you're the adventurous type and have a circle of friends with happy, social dogs, host a pooch party. You don't have to wait until Fido's birthday to organize a canine celebration. A simple afternoon paw-tea, with games and treats for the dogs and tea and cookies for your human guests, will do.

Incorporate a few friends to help manage activities, as I did when Carolyn arrived with her small, carry-in-a-tote-bag tot of a Bolonka, Zoey. The Bolonka is a rare toy-dog breed that originated in Russia and is known for its merrymaking qualities: friendly, sweet, loving, and eager to please, with a maximum weight of eleven pounds. Carolyn gave me the idea to make the baby-bottle treat dispenser, and I put her to work to show other pet parents how easy it is to construct. Our *pooch party on the patio* included a dozen dogs, selected for size and temperament, and was just as fun, if considerably less expensive, than any birthday party I hosted for my young son and his friends over the years. No need to hire magicians, balloon-making artists, or inflatable bounce castles. The dogs provide entertainment for each other!

Carolyn at our Pooch Party

Pooch Party on the Patio!

In addition to fraternizing with other dogs, your dog needs regular outdoor forays with a myriad of new smells and terrain to explore. This is critical to your dog's physical and mental health. A bored or lonely dog will exhibit unwanted behavior at home to send you their message.

Don't be discouraged if your dog isn't hip to socializing with strangers or in public places at first. Many certified professional dog trainers can help you ease them into new situations.

Every dog, regardless of breed or age, can be a party animal. It's up to the owner to unleash it.

CHAPTER THIRTY
ACTION JACKSON—THE LIFE OF THE PARTY

It's always an entertaining adventure with uber social dogs. A stand-up canine comic routine always occurred when Jackson, a Shih Tzu-Coton de Tulear mix, came to stay. I met Jackson and his parents, Herb and Marti, when he was only six months old; he quickly earned the nickname Action Jackson. Herb and Marti were friends with Bill and Virginia, owners of a purebred Shih Tzu, Brandy. Bill will tell you that Brandy isn't entirely purebred: she's 80% Shih Tzu and 20% jackrabbit!

As these friends frequently traveled together, Jackson and Brandy came to my house as a package deal. This dynamic duo played together like a couple in love. Their interaction was joyful and playful. They didn't stop to rest, and neither did I.

Typically, when well-mannered, socially balanced dogs meet, they have a little party in the yard, yet they'll naturally take periodic time-outs. Not these two! They ran and chased each other, or anything else that moved or made noise, all day long. They were pups with a bipartisan approach and happily included other dogs in their playgroup.

The Shih Tzu is well known as a charming lapdog with a sanguine attitude, playfulness, and fondness for its family, children, and other dogs. Officially known as the Shih Tzu Kou, meaning Lion Dog, its origins are associated with China, although they were also known in Tibet, where they were considered to be holy dogs.

Brandy had her own special traits, which included the desire to swim—in the water dish. She would dive into the smallest of bowls and paddle with her paws. Her holy baptismal moments were a first for me, yet I didn't mind the small ponds on my tile floor, as she was so engaging.

After crashing at the end of the day, Brandy would promptly rise at 6:00 a.m., trot to the door to the outdoors, sit, and stare. Most dogs need to pee first thing. Brandy didn't budge an inch. All the encouragement I could muster didn't make a difference. I was flummoxed by this; still, she never had an accident in the house. Her bladder control was amazing for such a young dog, yet I later learned it was simply her "potty" protocol.

In casual conversation, I was advised that her parents walked her every morning at 6:00 a.m. She expected a leash and an outdoor stroll, despite having the largest outhouse in my backyard.

She had her pick of my 7,000 square feet of either grass or gravel, and still she was a no-go (literally). Ugh. I'm not a morning person. With a super-charged cup of coffee in hand, I satisfied my little charge with a daily walk around the block. Clearly, this was another lesson regarding the importance of maintaining a dog's daily routines and expectations.

As these two amped-up pups matured, they continued to grace my home, allowing me to nap in the afternoon for longer than five minutes, and eventually Brandy retired her swim fins.

These pet parents did everything right. They met every day with other neighbors and their dogs to fraternize and exercise. As a result, both Jackson and Brandy matured into well-balanced, socially active dogs.

Curiously enough, while Jackson was a well-mannered houseguest for several years, an unusual detour occurred in his behavior. On one particular staycation, his parents arrived to announce that, out of the blue, he'd begun marking indoors. Not in their home, mind you, as he is an only child; yet, for some reason, Jackson felt compelled to mark in the house of a friend (who had other dogs). They were mortified and apologetic, yet they fully disclosed this new behavior, which did not create any alarm on my part. Okay then! Let's get this party started and see what happens next.

As described and disclosed, he lifted his leg on my baseboard within minutes of check-in. I responded with a quick "ah-ah-ah!" and a swift escort outdoors. When this did not deter him from continued watering of my baseboards and walls, out came the pet diapers. For three days, he wore disposable doggie diapers indoors, removed when outside to eliminate like a big boy, and outfitted with a fresh diaper once brought back inside.

Much to my surprise, on the fourth day of this new routine, Jackson froze while looking at me with a fresh diaper in my hand. Something about his reticent stance and the look in his eye said, "I don't want to do this anymore."

I promise you, his body language spoke volumes. I decided to trust my interpretation and put the diaper away. I gave him the freedom to prove he would be a polite guest again. He immediately stopped these leg-lifting moments. I cannot explain what caused his temporary diversion from outdoor marking to indoor target practice. I can assure you that with patience and understanding, if not a very short-term solution, Jackson got the message, and so did I. Sometimes, we just act up and need a little redirection to get back on track.

CHAPTER THIRTY-ONE
WHAT WENT WRONG?

Despite the best efforts of all pet parents, some things can't be explained. You might be that dedicated owner who has done everything right; you acquired your puppy, read all the books, enrolled her in early socialization and obedience classes, provided endless love and early exposure to new experiences including other people and pets. And yet, your dog has a quirk.

If unusual phobias or bizarre reactions to ordinary situations send your dog into a tailspin, don't panic. Every one of us has a fear of something; whether rational or not, we can conquer it.

Such was the case with Emma, a delightful 35-pound Sheltie who came to stay about the time I thought I was the end-all for dogs. Her mom told me she was on the shy side, common for Shelties, yet I was in no way prepared for this level of skittishness.

The Shetland Sheepdog originated in the Shetland Islands of Scotland as a herding dog and provided the stock for latter-day Collies, although in the isolation of these islands, the breed developed quickly and with purity. They are sensitive, willing to please, and supremely devoted to family. However, they can be reserved or timid around strangers, as I soon discovered.

Despite a successful introduction in advance, with Mom present, Emma arrived for her four-day staycation and spent the first two days hiding behind a living room chair.

Betty brought a crate for Emma's comfort, and while I advocated cage-free boarding, with no intention of crating her, I needed that apparatus as a vessel for her food and water. While she hid in the living room, away from all dog and human activity, I knew I had to get her outside eventually to potty!

I tried everything, yet despite my best efforts, this shy girl wanted nothing to do with me.

Following frequent reconnaissance checks to ensure her food and water levels were both ample and consumed, I simply let her be. I had little choice but to give her all the space she needed and not overreact; yet my teeth were swimming for her.

Finally, she emerged to join us outdoors—I'm sure due to the call of nature, which promoted her appearance. It was such a relief for both of us, I danced a bit with personal excitement and praise for her. She immediately ran back inside to the sanctity of her now-claimed safe space.

As we communicate daily with our pet parents, my eureka-moment text was simply: "There's been an Emma sighting."

Much to my delight, after the second day, she joined the pack on the dog-sanctioned and guest-occupied futon. While she didn't stay there long, it was a big step for this little girl who showed her phobia in a new place with strange people and other dogs. Once Emma was comfortable with this new arrangement, we were finally able to go for a walk together, as she stood by the front door with enough confidence to harness up.

Emma was acquired as a puppy, with no prior history of abuse or unusual confrontation. She was introduced to various people and other pets along the way and was an otherwise aptly socialized dog. It's possible that something happened in the breeder's home that triggered a deep-rooted memory in my home or she was overwhelmed by the presence of many dogs at one time—despite our 3,000 square feet and plenty of distance from the other dogs. It was simply a quirk that required patience, understanding, and acceptance that she was a normal dog just outside her norm. Emma finally accepted us as "safe ground" after two days together. Most dogs take two hours or less.

Emma eventually grew out of this hide-and-no-peek phase and continues to board with us without reservation and with only moderate shyness. She simply needed more time to find her compass when navigating new places.

Her true north is undoubtedly with her parents, Betty and Larry, yet we're happy she has accepted us as alternate family when Betty and Larry travel. She continues to walk confidently beside us.

CHAPTER THIRTY-TWO
WALK THIS WAY

With multiple dogs coming and going daily, I unpacked their luggage and spread it out in segments across the kitchen counter. In addition to a medley of food, treats, and toys, walking accessories are often included. I was operating a cage-free pet resort, yet structurally it was similar to a kindergarten classroom outfitted with individual cubby spaces for possessions storage and plans for daytime activities, which included walks for my furry charges.

The amazing ensemble of dazzling retail variety included head halters, gentle leaders, "collars-for-walking-only," leashes in every color and length, and body harnesses.

While saddling up for a walk, with a pack of dogs overly excited about the prospect of an outdoor foray, I would spend half an hour corralling these unpenned and eager guests while also configuring the attire—a gentle leader, loose collars that required another notch for safety, and myriad harnesses. Each had to be assembled individually, and some required an engineer's degree to figure out. Sadly, there was the occasional prong or shock collar packed for the ill-trained.

As I don't believe in using forceful collars, I invested in doggie day packs for the runners and pullers. Weighted with water bottles, the simple addition of a pack on their back gives the dog a "job" and added sense of responsibility: "You want me to carry this for you? I must be important. You've got my attention." With the added weight of small water bottles balanced on both sides, it's like power walking with hand weights. It's a slightly more intense workout at a slower pace for these dogs.

I quickly abandoned the use of retractable leashes. While cleverly marketed in a beautiful rainbow of colors, they are an absolute nightmare. It's a mini guillotine at the end of a handle.

The cord itself acts like a bullwhip if you are suddenly required to pull on it to get your dog back to you quickly. This assumes you are in control of the various buttons that manage the extension feature of the leash. Sometimes the push button wouldn't work and the leash failed to retract. I thought it was just blonde me and not a malfunctioning leash, worn by time. Worse, with up to 26 feet of extension, the dogs could run into the street or encounter another dog, leaving me very little control to avoid potential dangers.

Given the freedom to run with less restraint, dogs can easily become tangled in the cord. Humans can get tied up too, and it's all too easy to get a leg burn or a cut in the process. My son, Nash, discovered this one day when I sent him out with one large, boisterous dog on a retractable leash. He came home with a nasty bleeding cut around his ankle. My son took it on the shin, and I learned another lesson: ditch this leash.

A properly fitting harness is the safest way to walk your dog. With a bull ring attachment at the chest or back, there is little chance your dog can wiggle out of his collar and run with abandon.

For many dogs, a harness also serves as a quasi-backpack and might give them the added sense of responsibility to walk respectfully. Leash training, of course, is the safest and best bet.

I like to refer to the easy-to-walk dogs as *high-heel worthy*. If you can confidently walk your dog in high heels, with little or no concern of personal injury, you know you've done a good job leash training your dog. This is hypothetical, of course, as you should always don your tennies when walking your dog.

Remember, your shoe is a visual clue to your dog, signaling the excitement that follows your Nike wardrobe-changing moment. And your dog may be great on a leash, until a bunny appears.

CHAPTER THIRTY-THREE
THE SCOOP ON POOP!

An often-overlooked accessory when walking a dog is the poop bag. I appreciate responsible dog owners who actually pocket a plastic grocery bag or purchase a handy poo-bag attachment for their dog's leash; far too many folks are under the false impression that their dog's doo will magically self-destruct if left in the open.

After ten years in the pet-care business, with tens of thousands of dog walks logged in virtually every local zip code, it is grossly obvious to me that many dog owners have complete disregard for picking up after their pet. This blithe ignorance is universally witnessed in open public spaces, parks, sidewalks, and residential lawns. Even more curious is the marginal effort to actually bag it before walking away empty-handed.

Leaving pet waste on the ground increases public health risks, as harmful bacteria and nutrients will wash into storm drains and local water systems.

To dispel any preconceived notions about the breakdown of a dog's abandoned litter, please know that dog waste takes at least a year to decompose and is NOT a good source of natural fertilizer. The process of making fertilizer is very complicated, involving many materials harvested over time. Cat and dog feces are not standalone fertilizing components unless composted with other materials that will break it down over time, which only happens in a commercial plant.

Hopscotching around fallen "debris" is never fun for those who wish to enjoy an unfettered landscape and can be hazardous to a dog's health, as well as ours.

Many harmful diseases can be transmitted to animals and humans through infected feces. Dogs can both spread and contract parvovirus, Coronavirus, Leptospirosis, Giardia, roundworms, heartworms, hookworms, tapeworms, whipworms, salmonella, and E. coli through their dung. It is estimated that 1 gram of dog waste contains *23 million fecal coliform bacteria.*

You should never let your dog sniff or step on public poop, given these potential diseases lying in wait.

Another reason to properly remove your pup's poop in public is to minimize the flies. Flies love it, lay eggs in it, and eventually find their way through open doors and windows, typically landing on the kitchen counter. Doolittle's nannies are prepared to stand guard in the backyard *with catcher's mitts* to ensure swift removal and proper disposal of guests' waste.

There isn't a single argument that can be made for the insubordination of those who defy local ordinances and these public health issues. "I forgot to bring a bag" won't cut it. As the saying goes: "Haste makes waste."

Every responsible dog-owning citizen should be prepared in advance. If you left your poop bags at home and get caught on your walk with an empty hand as you stare at your dog's business, return to the scene of the crime later, if at all possible. If this happens in the woods, while glamping with your dogs, bury it.

Local ordinances exist in every county, city, and state, with fines ranging from $100–$500 for offenders caught in the act. Enforcement is virtually non-existent and difficult to employ.

Posting individual notices both publicly and privately might keep sign merchants in business yet seems to do very little to deter errant dog owners from upholding their civic doo-ty.

It is an absolute and non-negotiable responsibility of every dog owner to remove their dog's public waste. Some may simply be too embarrassed to carry around a less-than-sexy bag of bounty swinging from side to side. A fashionable and discreet product cleverly designed to pack it away is the Go Two Bag pouch, a "trash can on the go."

These fabulous creations are made of waterproof material, include two side pockets (with snap closures) to hold house keys (or hand sanitizer) on one side and a roll of disposal bags on the other. This affordable carrier combines practicality with pizazz. It's sanitary and convenient, and it attaches to your dog's leash; you can find these for $20 at https://www.gotwobag.com; with an additional $5 off as a special offer for our readers. This is a small price to pay for artful prudence while freeing up your hands until a receptacle for proper disposal can be located.

The most environmentally friendly way to dispose of dog poop is to flush it down your toilet. This only works at home, so when walking your dog in public, consider biodegradable bags as an added eco-friendly measure.

I'm proud to carry my second-use plastic grocery bags while out walking dogs and gladly *stoop to scoop* as a good sanitation-minded citizen. Please share these eco-minded facts with anyone who will spread the news within their community that the blatant disregard of fecal discard is a public health problem that goes far beyond the obstacle it creates on the sidewalk.

CHAPTER THIRTY-FOUR
DOGS WHO OUTLIVE THEIR PARENTS

The most overlooked facet of pet ownership is undoubtedly the need to appoint a guardian to care for them when you can't.

I shall never forget the bittersweet pleasure of hosting Bridgette, a well-cared-for and genteel King Charles Cavalier, who lived a life of royalty with her parents.

The King Charles Cavalier is also referred to as English Toy Spaniel. Their popularity soared in England during the reign of King Charles, and they were popular among the wealthy classes as foot and lap warmers. These are gentle, quiet and calm dogs.

Early boarding experiences were booked when her parents' pleasure trips couldn't include Bridgette. I gladly shared my lap and bed, as a temporary replacement for the pampered moments she enjoyed at home and had been accustomed to for eleven years.

She was an easy dog to host with little demand and complete complacency on her part. There is no perfect dog, as none of us are perfect, yet Bridgette was a five-star guest in all regards.

The next assignment would be required when Mom went to the hospital. While her boarding experience was no different than in the past, this one extended almost three weeks. Bridgette was grateful to return home when Mom was released from treatment.

One year later, I got the call: Bridgette needed boarding as Mom had passed. Could I keep her for an indefinite amount of time while the family mourned and prepared for her memorial?

Incredibly saddened by this family's loss, I offered free pet taxi service and, after visiting with the bereaved, departed with Bridgette and her accessories. I had the uncomfortable feeling that she would not be returning home this time.

That intuition proved spot on when the heirs eventually asked me to find a home for Bridgette. Following the settlement of affairs, it became apparent that no family member wanted to be Bridgette's new parent.

While I often wondered if desperate pet parents might book a boarding gig and never return for their dog, this had never happened, yet I was now in the regrettable situation of having to rehome a furry client. Now thirteen and accustomed to complete luxury, Bridgette was suddenly and unexpectedly homeless.

This was a brand-new experience for me; I'm grateful it was an isolated event. While rescue groups spend every day rehoming abandoned pets, this was beyond my purview. In a fretful flummox, I started chatting with nannies, friends, and clients. My frenetic "barking" led me to a family with two Cavaliers who had an interest in adopting Bridgette.

Following several conversations with them and a two-hour interview—allowing interaction between Bridgette and her potential siblings—Bridgette was welcomed into the Cotter's home, and I left with a happy heart.

I have undying gratitude to Susan and Ed for their incredible love in embracing Bridgette as a new family member, despite her senior status at time of arrival.

Bridgette Finds a New Family

Not all dogs who outlive their parents have such a happy ending. The sad reality is that very few of us think to appoint a guardian for our beloved pets, much less include them in a trust or will.

As hard as it might be to imagine life without your pet, please consider how hard it might be for your pet to live without you.

As this is a ruff subject to ponder, the following guidelines are offered for serious consideration to all pet parents. It's a tough pill to swallow yet a critically important one to digest and implement.

1. Name a guardian in your will who has agreed to accept the role of caregiver for your pet.

2. Establish a trust (or provision in an existing trust) providing distributions to cover your pet's entire needs and expenses. *Pet trusts are legally recognized in all fifty states and the District of Columbia.*

3. Provide detailed instructions pertaining to your pet's specific needs and define requirements for the caregiver to submit expenses for reimbursement (if a trustee is involved).

4. Consider your pet's standard of living and life expectancy in order to determine the appropriate amount of money to set aside for their lifetime needs. Be sure to add administrative costs if a trustee is involved.

5. Consult with your insurance agent about adding your pet to existing life insurance policies that cover your human family.

6. If you are unable to establish a will or trust that includes your pets, consider other caregivers, such as family members, close friends, or trusted neighbors—preferably someone who has a relationship with your pet. It will be important to have a meaningful conversation with your appointed caregiver so they are fully aware of the responsibility and cost involved.

7. A periodic update may be necessary to ensure that lifestyle changes still allow your designated caregiver to assume responsibility if needed. For example, if your neighbor or family member moves, acquires their own pets or children, experiences a job change that creates financial burden, or encounters some other incapacity to care for your pet. Despite best intentions, "life happens," and these informal arrangements may need to be reconsidered.

8. If you don't have someone close to you who will assume responsibility, consider consulting with a local shelter or rescue organization. Setting aside funds will help tremendously should you designate a shelter as your pet-care provider. Visit 2ndchanceforpets.org and check out their Resources section for a list of animal sanctuaries and perpetual care programs

that may be another solution if you do not have anyone who can act as your pet's guardian.

9. Carry an Emergency Contact card in your wallet that alerts emergency-response personnel to the pets in your home who may be left alone. All pet owners should have emergency information available in their home as well, in the event of a household disaster that requires sudden evacuation. For our valued readers, we have provided a tear-out version to complete, fold, and carry with you.

10. We have a special link on our website, published with permission from 2ndchanceforpets.org, that includes a downloadable guide you can complete and review with the person you trust to care for your pet when you can't. You can access it directly at https://doolittlesdoghouse.com/resources-guides/.

Pets in our home

Our phone number

Our name

Emergency Contact Information

DOGHOUSE
doolittle's

-------- fold here --------

Veterinarian

Name _____

Phone number _____

Emergency Pet Caregivers

Name _____

Phone number _____

Name _____

Phone number _____

Please copy this template and share with a friend! Update when phone #'s or names change for your Emergency Pet Caregivers

✂ cut here

Emergency Contact Information card can be downloaded here:

https://doolittlesdoghouse.com/resources-guides

CHAPTER THIRTY-FIVE
BONDING FOR BETTER HEALTH

Much has been written about the human-dog bond and the health benefits pets provide. Multiple studies support the positive outcomes, both physical and emotional, that result from owning a pet or simply spending time with one.

We exercise more when we exercise dogs, while also benefitting from social interaction along the way. We fraternize with other dog owners due to a common bond, not only at the dog parks, but also via social media, where we connect with each other digitally and proudly tweet, tout, and share funny videos of our furry kids.

We live longer, and happier, when pets are in the home. The therapeutic relationship between us encompasses every generation from child to elder.

Our cholesterol and blood pressure levels are lowered, and our oxytocin levels elevated in their presence. Pets give us an added sense of purpose and a renewed leash on life.

In addition to the "feel-good" psychological and physical enhancements a dog promotes, many scientists are now looking at the probiotic effect of good dog-gut bacteria that may boost our immune systems as well. This physiological correlation, referred to as the *hygiene hypothesis*, is currently under scientific study across the country. The objective is to determine if humans may benefit from the micro bacteria that animals bring into our homes that then move into our digestive tracts.

Many hospitals, senior care centers, hospice professionals, child crisis group homes, and countless other organizations have incorporated pet therapy into their treatment programs to provide additional healing for their patients, residents, and families.

Autism Speaks is a family service offering a wide array of resources for parents and children living with disabilities. Their website offers an encyclopedia of helpful guidance in broad categories including several service dog organizations they recommend. This includes Autism Service Dogs of America, 4 Paws for Ability, Assistance Dogs International, and others that recognize the inherent value and healing power of therapy-trained assistance dogs.

Pets for Vets is a "home run" organization connecting shelter pets waiting for forever homes with our military service members returning home from war to civilian life, over 20% of whom suffer from PTSD and physical difficulties. It's a grand slam—the companion animal escapes the crowded shelter and receives professional training while going to bat for the brave soldier who needs a devoted furry fan to navigate life's new bases.

The initiative was founded in 2009 by Executive Director Clarissa Black. This superhero paired her extensive skills and studies in animal behavior and training with both the veteran and the animal at the core of her Super Bond™ matching program. Using only positive reinforcement training methods she developed, her work benefits both vet and pet, based on mutual trust and respect; she never advocates using force.

Soldier's Best Friend operates in Arizona. With an impressive staff of trainers, veterinarians, volunteers, and corporate sponsors, their programs are available to all U.S. military veterans, living with combat-related PTSD or TBI, who wish to apply for a therapy-trained companion animal.

Combat stress, PTSD, Traumatic Brain Injury (TBI), and physical injury are the unfortunate consequences faced by many of our brave military men and women after serving their country in war-torn places you and I will never experience nor can possibly imagine.

Pets on Wheels of Scottsdale is a visiting therapy dog organization serving 35+ health care centers in Scottsdale. They have 110 volunteers who, along with their dogs, visit cancer patients and elderly residents for an hour or more each week.

Board of Directors member John Grizzard and his dog, Cooper, have logged over 350 visits together at various senior care centers and the Virginia G. Piper Cancer Center in Scottsdale, Arizona. John and Cooper have also been certified to participate in the new Phoenix Sky Harbor Airport program "Navigator Buddies." This program uses therapy dogs with their handlers to navigate within the Phoenix International Airport terminals to comfort stressed-out passengers.

American Humane is a well-established national network of broad-reaching programs to promote not only the human-animal bond but also the welfare and safety of children, and the human and animal condition.

Founded in 1877, with the initial task of addressing the inhumane treatment of farm animals, American Humane has amassed an impressive history of successful advocacy programs ranging from animal rescue in disasters and cruelty cases to promoting a humane Hollywood by governing the treatment of animal actors, ensuring safe and humane treatment of all farm animals, establishing conservation programs, and serving the military on all sides of the fence. Their Pups4Patriots™ program provides therapy training for qualified shelter pets in order to unchain their suppressed potential so they can administer the healing power of their paws to help their new owners cope with civilian life.

These specific organizations, and countless others not mentioned, are firmly rooted in the value of embracing all animals that naturally promote human health and healing.

CHAPTER THIRTY-SIX
INTRODUCING YOUR BOYFRIEND OR GIRLFRIEND TO THE FAMILY DOG

In other matters of the heart, dating is always fun when you own a pet, if not a gauge in compatibility. In those early years, with ten dogs running around, my prospective paramours were carefully prepared in advance. The blind dates were the funniest, as they knocked on my door and a cacophony of canine alert ensued. For those brave enough to stick around, the dogs became my litmus test to their desirability as a suitor. There were a few that bolted instead.

When attending a black-tie affair was involved, I would meet my date in the driveway so his tuxedo didn't capture dog hair as an unintentional accessory. I routinely dispensed lint rollers as party favors to friends who came to visit. Any gentleman who didn't appreciate dogs or showed visible signs of aversion in their presence was shown the proverbial doghouse. *Must love dogs* is an absolute for me as my world is wrapped in their paws. For other singles, it's much easier to coax a bond when it's just you and them.

If you love dogs and your soon-to-be-significant other doesn't, the adage that "opposites attract" isn't likely. You can improve the outcome and overcome both canine and new-companion reticence by keeping a few key tips in mind.

You know your dog best. If yours is the type to greet everyone enthusiastically, then you have little to worry about when they meet your date.

However, for the shy, skittish, or fearful dog, use the "Treat and Retreat" method upon introduction. Assuming your dog is food motivated, have treats on hand and ask your new friend to dispense as instructed when they first meet. For most dogs, the way to their heart starts with their stomach.

To further develop a pack relationship, consider planning a few dates that include your dog. A picnic in the park, long walks, having dinner at a dog-friendly restaurant (patio dining for three), or attending local dog-friendly events together are just a few ideas to build your new team.

Once your dog accepts your new friend as part of his tribe, you should be able to spend more time away without him resenting this "intruder." Pay attention to your dog's reactions. If he isn't accepting this new person and continues to act warily despite your best efforts to bond them, he may be telling you something you need to know about the "chemistry" in the offing.

CHAPTER THIRTY-SEVEN
INTRODUCING A BABY TO YOUR DOG

Introducing your newborn to your dog is a much bigger endeavor that requires considerable planning in advance. While you can choose to dive into or ditch a romantic relationship, babies are permanent family additions, and creating romance between your infant and furry child is critical.

The planning can start at conception! Start by playing tape recordings of baby sounds so your dog can get used to the shift in noises that will accompany baby's arrival. Invest early in the diaper disposal bin, baby lotions, wipes, and powders, and introduce these new smells to your dog in advance.

Begin simulation of new-life motions by walking your dog with an empty stroller, rocking in the empty chair you plan to use for baby, and standing at the changing table and pretending to diaper your baby.

You may decide to keep your dog out of the baby's room, especially if they can scale the crib out of curiosity, excitement, or desire to get really close to your little miracle. Your dog, however, should not be relegated to extreme confinement or isolation once your baby moves in. Establish in advance his own retreat room where baby will not encroach.

Including your dog in the daily activities of nursing and rocking a baby to sleep can be accomplished with a little training ahead of time. Designate a special "go-to" place in the same room the baby will occupy. Provide a pet bed or mat and teach him to "Go there" by standing next to the pet pad and providing a treat each time he complies. Then establish a release command ("Okay! Release!") and toss a treat so he has to leave the mat to retrieve it. Repeat this process, gradually increasing the time he stays on the mat so he learns to sit or lie down patiently in this special spot in the baby's room. This will encourage positive family interaction by including your dog in the daily marathon of round-the-clock baby care.

Just before you bring your new charge home from the hospital, let your dog sniff the baby's blanket or clothing for the smell about to permeate the home. You should greet your dog alone before entering with your swaddled bundle. You want to slowly introduce them and maintain cautious distance for a few days as your dog adjusts. Allow your dog to approach the baby when he's ready, and do not overreact with fear or "shoo" him away when he does. You need to be calm and controlled during that first sniff. You want your dog to accept this new member in the household and be confident that he hasn't lost his place in the family tree. Continue to praise and provide daily affection to your dog. You'll be busy with baby and undoubtedly sleep deprived in the first several weeks. If Fido is ignored in the process, he might resent this "new kid on the block" and act out in his own childish or unwanted way.

Buy a new toy for your dog so he has his own comfort object that is dazzling and different. A puzzle toy or hard-chew stick can be used to entertain your dog while you nurse or rock your baby. Don't punish your dog if he plays with baby's toys. Simply exchange the forbidden toy with one of his. Provide dog treats while feeding your baby. Take walks together as a family. If you can't manage a daily walk jostling a stroller or baby sling, poo bags, and beverage bottles, hire a dog walker.

You want your dog to make positive associations with baby inter-action. When your baby is sleeping, don't lavish attention and go *guilt-ridden overboard* with your dog when it's quiet. When baby cries (her own howls to signal a need), toss treats at your dog at the same time. The idea is to create the expectation that when baby is awake and vocal, fun things happen!

Be prepared that once your dog accepts this cooing, booing, and pooing marvel of nature, your child will start crawling, grabbing at things, and moving faster than before. While this represents a new period of adjustment, the good news is the continued elevation of the baby from parents' arms to a high chair isn't far behind. Once in the high chair, food will fly; your dog will benefit from the launch of Cheerios, valuing even more this new food source.

A mountain of YouTube videos and Internet photos capture the family dog "babysitting" or sleeping with an infant. Those marvelous and *awwww* moments demonstrate the unique relationship that can develop between your kids—both those with two and four legs. However, no matter how well your dog and baby get along, for safety's sake the two should never be left alone together unsupervised.

If you struggle with the juggle, contact a professional pet trainer to help you with a private consultation in your home. This may be necessary when the time comes to teach your child how to properly interact with and touch the family dog ... pencils up the nose and all.

CHAPTER THIRTY-EIGHT

SEPARATION ANXIETY—IT'S NORMAL!

You are everything to your dog. They want to be in your presence every single moment, regardless of the room you occupy—including the bathroom and, in some instances, inside the shower (let me bathe with you, please!) We've seen it. It's not that unusual, though it's not recommended that you allow your superglued-to-you dog bathe with you. However, if you are the type to multi-task with your pet while you're both in the loo, using your one free hand to dispense a back scratch, you're not alone.

Just know that when your dog is separated from you, he or she might exhibit some form of anxiousness regardless of the amount of time you are apart. Even a quick trip to the store usually prompts the happy dance when you return, as if your dog were saying, "Why were you gone so long?"

I love the owners who describe their dogs as "Velcro" attached. I'm here to tell you that they attach to us like Velcro too. It's our mission to provide emotional attachment with our canine families.

This is the richly rewarding human-dog bond we strive for, and we know you do too.

While some breeds are naturally aloof, and not as disturbed by our periodic absences, it is a common reaction for most dogs to miss their owners when they leave, as expressed by panting, whining, barking, looking at the door you just exited, or pacing back and forth.

It's been our continued experience that within just a few hours, our furry guests settle in and begin to play. As the majority of our first-time clients become repeats, the initial separation anxiety often dissipates completely as they race to our doors with wagging tails, in anticipation of a happy staycation experience. A little whining at first is easily assuaged by soothing tones and praise, without overt fawning. We remind guests how much fun we are by setting out our baskets of new toys and making our home environments rich with different smells and landscapes to explore. An immediate walk often helps the anxious guests relieve their energy through exercise and play with other dogs upon arrival.

Consider that each dog we host has observed their owners packing for a trip. The suitcase comes out, and their owner rushes around to complete necessary chores before leaving town. In the frantic days that often precede a trip, a dog's routines may be slightly altered. There may be less time for a walk, or the owner may be traveling under duress, perhaps to care for a sick relative or make a bereavement visit. Human emotional upset is also felt by dogs. Even the most balanced, happy dog can suddenly develop separation anxiety following a dramatic change in their daily routines.

If you've moved recently, divorced them from a loved one, transitioned from working at home to an office job, or undergone a similar game-changing event, your dog will naturally react with some agitation or mild depression.

In cases of extreme separation anxiety or unusual attachment, intentional urination, destruction, howling, or attempts to flee may present. It is not recommended that you crate your overly anxious dog because she is suddenly tearing up the drywall or your designer pillows to relieve anxiety. If you haven't crate-trained your dog in the past and she isn't used to being confined, this new barrier may cause worse damage, as your dog attempts to escape the crate, injuring herself in the process.

Neither can you punish her after the fact for making a mess in the house while you were gone. Begin in-home training by desensitizing your dog to the visual cues that you are about to leave. Grab your purse and car keys and leave the house for only a few minutes then promptly return. Do not make a big deal about your dog's ecstatic reaction when she sees you. Wait until she settles and sits before you praise and pet. Repeat this exercise often, gradually increasing the time you are gone. Continue to provide daily exercise and mental enrichment. You've heard it said countless times: "A tired dog is a happy dog."

Ideally, your dog trusts that you will return and will be able to occupy herself while you're away. This assumes that you are not leaving your dog home alone for extended periods of time.

We maintain a "no more than four-hour-long absence" rule when guests are in our home. As it is impossible to provide 24/7 attention, we limit our time for off-site errands, with absolute certainty that our guests will be comfortable alone for up to four hours. If we are boarding a puppy or highly anxious dog, this timeframe is reduced. Longer periods of time left alone will cause loneliness, boredom, and destructive behaviors that can't be blamed on the dog. You might consider adding another dog to your family to provide companionship while you're away.

Always consult with a professional trainer or certified canine behaviorist to assist you when you've tried everything and nothing seems to help. A veterinary exam may also be necessary to rule out any underlying medical conditions that might be the cause of dramatic change in your dog's behavior.

CHAPTER THIRTY-NINE
PEACEFUL PASSING

While we devote our lives to our pets, receiving equal faithfulness in return, the inevitable and painful end to our journey together will arrive. It will be one of your worst days ever when you are permanently separated from each other. If you've been forced into a decision to euthanize while in the sterile room of an after-hours emergency clinic, know that there is an alternative. Planning for your pet's passing in advance is a more peaceful option and spares tremendous pain and suffering for both you and your dog.

For most of us, it's hard to know when that time has arrived. We feel guilty about assuming the role of God. We can't be sure if Fido still has good days ahead. He seems content, so we wait for a sign. How do you know when it's time to let go and say goodbye?

Short answer: you don't really. Your veterinarian can help in this regard, especially if you have an open, honest, and deep relationship between you, your vet, and your pet.

Many veterinarians have expanded their services to include a designated "chapel" in their clinic for these private moments. And some veterinarians are mobile, dedicated to helping you with a final celebration and making the last day the best it can be under the circumstances.

Having personally lost my last two companions in an ER room, due to undiagnosed conditions that presented in the worst way, I would give my invisible dew claws to rewind and do it over. I would hold my dog in the comfort of my arms in our home, with family and friends present following a big, fat steak dinner for them, the scene set with candles and soft music.

While I didn't have that privilege, and the amount of tissues needed would have been the same, I would not have the lingering and painful memory of those final moments. It's such a helpless feeling. If only I'd known, I would have provided a more peaceful farewell.

Consider the following suggestions to help you discern when you've reached that painful point:

1. Make a list of your dog's good days versus bad, noting the things that your dog normally likes to do and whether these joyful events are noticeably absent.

2. Are they hiding in new places not normally frequented before or seeking refuge in a new area of the yard? This is often a sign of pain or a precursor to your dog's preparation for crossing over, referred to as "denning."

3. Have they stopped eating or drinking for an extended period?

4. Are they continually vomiting after eating?

5. Are they chronically whimpering or crying? If vocalization has escalated beyond normal, your dog may be in intense pain.

6. Are they able to walk without collapsing?

7. Are they unable to relieve themselves due to immobility or the lack of desire to get up and go?

8. Are they able to breathe normally? Unusually labored breathing is an antecedent to monitor closely.

9. Are they experiencing muscle spasms, tremors, or chronic shaking? Digestive disruption accompanied by a change in

eating patterns will manifest in bodily quivers.

10. Does your dog have cancer or an acute illness?

When your heart beats so strongly for your dog that you are paralyzed by emotion, indecision, your own rationale, or finances, it's okay to talk to friends and family, and it's okay to pray. Pray for a sign it's time and the strength and courage to end their suffering. Some pet owners are blessed when their beloved pets pass naturally in their sleep. How fortunate and graceful, if so lucky.

For those who've been advised by their trusted veterinarian that your time together is now short, throw a final celebration of life and help your dog or cat depart in peace.

I believe that our pets have souls and they are received and healed in heaven with the same glory as those beloved family members who've passed in our past. As quoted in the *Laudato Si*, by Pope Francis: "Eternal life will be a shared experience of awe, in which each creature, resplendently transfigured, will take its rightful place and have something to give those poor men and women who will have been liberated once and for all."[24]

May you find peace in your memories and the courage to gain another furry friend.

---

24 "Encyclical Letter Laudato Si' of the Holy Father Francis on Care for Our Common Home," http://w2.vatican.va/content/francesco/en/encyclicals/documents/papa-francesco_20150524_enciclica-laudato-si.html.

CHAPTER FORTY
NAMING YOUR FURBABY

When naming your new dog, it's often recommended that you keep it short, one to two syllables, and use hard consonants instead of soft ones (i.e., hard g in "garbage" versus the soft g in "gem"). You may want to avoid names that will frighten other people. "Killer," "Sid Vicious," and "Psycho" will not instill any confidence in others even though your tiny Yorkie poses little threat.

If there's a reluctant spouse in the house, let's not assume that naming your to-be-acquired dog after them will be the winning moment. Bill and Jill are great dog names, yet human Bill and Jill need a bigger buy-in. In the end, it is entirely up to you, and as all dogs should be treated like celebrities in the home, with entertaining names, let your imagination run wild.

While we've hosted a plethora of pooches with popular names, creative picks plucked from our private guest list include:

A: Abbey, Abigail, Ace, AJ, Ajax, Alfie, Allie, Amber, Angel, Annie, Apollo, April, Archie, Ares, Arlo, Arnold, Arthur, Arty, Assisi, Athena, Atlas

B: Baby, Baci, Bailey, Baja, Bambi, Banana, Bandit, Banjo, Barkley, Barnie, Batman, Baxter, Bay, Bear, Beau, Be-Be, Bella, Belle, Ben, Benji, Bennett, Benny, Bentley, Bert, Berta, Betsy, Bianca, Billy, Billy Ray, Biscuit, Bismarck, Bizou, Black Jack, Blaze, Blazer, Blu, Blue, Bob, Bobby, Bode, Bodhi, Bodie, Bodi O'Reilly, Bokkie, Bo, Bond, Boo, Booker, Boomer, Boss, Bowser, Brandy, Bridgette, Brodie, Bruce, Bruin, Brutus, Bubba, Buddie, Bug, Butters

C: Caesar, Caleb, Cali, Cammie, Capri, Captain, Cara, Casey, Cash, Casper, Ce-Ce, Chase, Chamois, Chandy, Chap, Charley, Cheddar, Cheeky, Chewy, Chloe, Chuck, Cinnamon, Cleopatra, Cloud, Clyde, Coco, Cocopah, Codie, Coffee, Cohen, Cohiba, Colby, Cole, Conner, Contessa, Cookie, Cooper, Corona, Cramer, Cricket, Cruiser, Cuddles

D: Daeneryas, Daisy, Daisy May, Dale, Dallas, Darby, Dash, Dayze, Decker, Dee Dee, Delilah, Denali, Dexter, Diablo, Diane, Digger, Dizzy, Dog, Dolce, Dood, Dorie, Doris, Dosido, Doug, Droid, Dublin, Dug, Duke

E: Earl, Edison, Edith, Eli, Ella, Ellie, Ellis, Elsa, Elway, Emery, Emi, Emma, Emmett, Emmie, Endo, Enzo, Ernie, Essy, Etto

F: Fausto, Fernando, Feta, Fifi, Finbar, Fiona, Fitz, Fonzie, Foxy, Frankie, Frazier, Freeman

G: Gabby, George, George Clooney, Georgie, Gidgette, Giggles, Gigi, Ginger, Ginny, Gizmo, Goldie, Grace, Gracie, Greer, Groucho, Gunner, Gus, Gus Gus, Gussie, Gypsy

H: Hagar, Hailey, Halle Berry, Hannah, Happy, Harley, Harper Lee, Harry Potter, Harvey, Hassie, Havac, Hector, Heidi, Heinrich, Henry, Herschel, Hiccup, Holly, Honey, Houston, Howie, Hudson, Hugster, Huxley

I: Ian, Ice, Illy, Indigo, Indy, Isabella, Iva

J: Jack, Jackie, Jackson, Jada, Jagger, Jake, Jameson, Jameson Gold, Jamie, Jasper, Jax, Jazzy, Jefferson, Jem, Jenny, Joe, Joey, Jo-Jo, Jorge, Josie, Junior, Juno

K: Kahlua, Kaia, Kaiya, Kali, Karma, Kasi, Katie, Keeva, Keller, Keno, Kenzie, Ki, Kia, Kiana, Kiki, Kiley, Kimmel, King, Kingsley, Kirby, Kismet, Kiwi, Koda, Kodak, Kodi, Kona, Kozmo, Krieger, Krypto

L: Lamar, Layla, Lea, Lee Bear, Leo, Levi, Libby, Lilly, Lina, Linus, Lizzie, Loki, Lola, Lolli, Lou, Louie, Luca, Lucia Havana, Lucy, Luigi, Lulu, Luna

M: Macho Man Randy Savage, Macie, Madison, Maggie, Maggie Moo, Maize, Makeeta, Malbec, Mama Bear, Mandy, Marco Polo, Margaux, Marley, Marshmallow, Mason, Mater, Maya, Max, Maxwell, Megan, Mia, Micah, Mickey, Mijo Joe, Mika, Millie, Milo, Mini, Miss Clara, Missy, Misty, Mochi, Mojito Bandito, Mojo, Mollie, Molly, Money Penny, Monty, Moose, Moxie, Mr. Green, Mulligan, Murphy, Mylo

N: Nala, Neeka, Neela, Nelka, Nelson, Nigel, Nika, Niko, Nina, Nori, Nova, Nugget

O: Oakley, Obie, Odin, Ojobo, Oliver, Ona, Oscar, Oso, Otis

P: Paco, Parker, Patch, Paulina, Payton, Peanut, Pearson, Pebbles, Pee Wee, Penny, Pepe, Pepper, Petey, Pi, Pico, Pierce, Pilot, Piper, Pippa, Pippin, Pipsqueak, Pixie, Poppy, Pork Chop, Porsche, Preston, Princess

Q: Quasimodo, Queenie, Quinn

R: Radar, Rago, Rags, Raider, Raife, Ramona, Ranger, Rascal, Reba, Reecie, Reese, Reggie, Remington, Remy, Reno, Renzo-Leon, Rex, Rhino, Riley, Rinty, Rio, Roady, Rocco, Rock, Rocky, Romeo, Roscoe, Rosey, Rosie, Rourke, Roxy, Royce, Rudy, Ruff, Rusty, Ruxin, Ruzzy, Ryno

S: Sabre, Saci, Sadie, Sako, Sam, Sammi, Sampson, Santana, Sasha, Sasha Bear, Scout, Scruffy, Scuji, Sedona, Serena, Shadow, Shakespeare, Shana, Sharona, Sharon, Shea, Sheila, Shelby, Sherman, Shorty, Si, Silver, Simba, Simon, Skeeter, Skipper, Skippy, Smedley, Snickers, Snuffy, Sookie, Sophia, Sophie, Spanky, Sparky, Spoon, Springer, Sprinkles, Spud, Spumoni, Star, Stella, Stevie, Stitch, Storm, Stormy, Streudel,

Sumesh, Summer, Sunny, Sunshine, Sushi, Susie, Sweet Besos, Sweet Pea, Sweetie, Sydney

T: Tabu, Taby, Taffy, Tana, Tank, Tasseau, Tater, Taz, Tea Toy, Teddy, Teddy Bear, Tella, Tessa, Thor, Tikki, Tobi, Toodles, Tootsie, Tori, Torque, Tortalina, Touche, Trey, Truckee, Truffle, Tsunami, Tuck, Tucker, Tula, Tyson, Tyson Wayne

V: Vanilla, Verona, Violet, Vito

W: Whiskey, Wiley, Willey, Willis, Willow, Winston, Wookie, Wyni

Y: Yadi, Yahoo, Yampa, Yang, Yeti, Yin, Yodi, Yogi

Z: Zadie, Zannah, Zeke, Ziggy, Ziva, Ziwi, Zoey, Zona, Zulka

Every dog, by any name, is a winner in our book. It is a joyful journey to have the pleasure of their company and their unending loyalty and comfort to us in our homes.

My Favorite Names

EPILOGUE

Arriving at the end of these precious pet stories, the most aptly written summation has been borrowed.

The original author is unknown yet best describes the divine nature of dogs and how we personally feel at Doolittle's Doghouse.

Why God Made Dogs

When God had made the Earth and Sky, the flowers and the trees,
He then made all the animals, and all the birds and bees.

And when His work was finished, not one was quite the same.
He said, "I'll walk the Earth of mine, and give each one a name."

And so He traveled land and sea, and everywhere He went,
a little creature followed Him, until its strength was spent.

When all were named upon the Earth, and in the sky and sea,
the little creature said,

"Dear Lord, there's not one left for me."

The Father smiled and softly said, "I've left you 'til the end, I've turned my name from back to front, and called you DOG, my friend."

THANK YOU ...

I hope you enjoyed reading about our walk with dogs, our best friends. We learn more about ourselves through our shared experiences, including the marvelous lessons taught by dogs when we pay attention to what they instinctively know and respond kindly to what they can teach us.

Simple life lessons to be learned from a dog:

Sit still. Enjoy every day. Smell each rose. Harmonize with nature. Make your mark on where you've been. Cock your ears to clearly hear the voices of others. Accept what is when it cannot be changed, yet do not hesitate to dig for more (just in case there's a hidden bone to be found). Take daily naps. Console the weak, injured, and emotionally distraught. Give lots of kisses and extend your paw; the world needs more hugs and sincere acts of kindness. Demonstrate forgiveness. Trust your instincts. Remain faithful to those who have earned your devotion. Look into the eyes of others. There's a soul and a story to be told in every gaze. Love unconditionally. Live, laugh, and howl happily often!

Thank you for your investment in this book and for your daily devotion to your dog. I hope you've learned something new, through our eyes and theirs.

Enjoy each day with your beloved pets in good health and happiness. God bless!

–Tori Levitt

ABOUT THE AUTHOR

Tori Levitt is the owner of Doolittle's Doghouse, a company of loving pet "nannies" with a corporate commitment to pampered pet care in a cage-free environment. Launched by happenstance in 2007, Tori followed her passion for animals, primarily focusing on dogs and cats that needed loving care while their owners traveled. Tori lives in Scottsdale, Arizona and continues to board other people's dogs while also providing Canine Concierge service with host accommodations for pet owners living in the Valley of the Sun. *The World According to Dog* is her contribution to animal lovers worldwide.

Join us on-line @ https://www.doolittlesdoghouse.com

Follow us on Facebook @ https://www.facebook.com/doolittlesdoghouse

Follow us on Twitter @ #DoolittlesDogHS

CPSIA information can be obtained
at www.ICGtesting.com
Printed in the USA
FSHW011954130319
56360FS